UFOs OVER BRITAIN

NEIL R. STOREY

AMBERLEY

First published 2025

Amberley Publishing
The Hill, Stroud
Gloucestershire, GL5 4EP

www.amberley-books.com

British Library Cataloguing in Publication Data.
A catalogue record for this book is available from the British Library.

ISBN 978 1 3981 2028 0 (hardback)
ISBN 978 1 3981 2029 7 (ebook)

1 2 3 4 5 6 7 8 9 10

Typesetting by SJmagic DESIGN SERVICES, India.
Printed in the UK.

Appointed GPSR EU Representative:
Easy Access System Europe Oü, 16879218
Address: Mustamäe tee 50, 10621, Tallinn, Estonia
Contact Details: gpsr.requests@easproject.com, +358 40 500 3575

UFOs
OVER BRITAIN

This book is dedicated to David Schrader, a dear friend and fellow traveller in the pursuit of mysteries and the truth.

Contents

Preface

When researching this book, I came across the scrapbooks compiled by Harry Lord, one of the founders of the Tyneside UFO Society and regular contributor to both *Orbit*, his own society's magazine, and *Flying Saucer Review*. Pasted into the front of the book is a foreword, clearly typed on a manual typewriter. To modern eyes it may seem overly dramatic and something more akin to a science-fiction novel, but it should be remembered it was written at a time when the Cold War was reaching its height and the world feared nuclear Armageddon. For Harry and most of those involved in the early years of UFO investigation, it also reflects an earnest belief in what they were doing and what they were dealing with. I have drawn on many of the stories loyally pasted by Harry onto the pages of his scrapbooks for this book and feel that after all these years languishing in a library store it should appear in a suitable volume. I hope Harry would have approved.

> This is a valuable record of occurrences connected with visits to this planet by unknown entities in flying saucers and other unidentified flying objects. It must not be destroyed or taken apart. It has been gathered together with the object of providing evidence of these occurrences and as proof of the reality of these strange objects and the events which probably relate to them.
>
> It is hoped that in the event of some major catastrophe to the world, this record and others like it will help to prevent the truth of these visits from becoming legends or myths to future survivors.
>
> Mankind as a whole first became aware of these objects from no one knows where, in the year 1947. I and others like me have concerned

ourselves with this activity and desire that the world should know the truth. We are ridiculed by those who cannot accept the concept of life on other worlds and dimensions. It is up to whoever acquires these records to value them and understand their full meaning.

Henry Bennett Lord
13 July 1960

Introduction

UFOs, or rather unexplained objects – they were described using a host of other names before the term UFO was invented – have been seen in the skies over Britain and around the world for centuries. However, the modern fascination with the anomalous craft occasionally seen in the sky above us began over in the USA with the sighting of nine unidentified craft in the air 'flipping and flashing in the sun just like a mirror' near Mount Rainier in the Cascade Range of mountains in the state of Washington by civilian pilot Kenneth Arnold on 24 June 1947. Arnold was quoted in the *Oregon Journal* of 27 June 1947 describing the craft he had seen as 'half-moon shaped, oval in front and convex in the rear ... I thought they might be jet planes, and I clocked them. Then when I saw they had no tails and I realized how fast they were going, I knew they were like nothing I had ever heard of before. There were no bulges or cowlings; they looked like a big flat disk. They were larger than the ordinary jet plane but slightly smaller than a DC4, if you don't count the rear fuselage.'

Arnold was also amazed at how the craft moved at an incredible speed (he estimated at being over 1,000 mph) 'like a saucer would if skipped across water'. The media lapped up the idea of 'Flying Saucers'; the story, to use modern parlance, went viral and many other people started reporting the strange objects they had spotted in the sky. The United States Air Force instigated research and reports on the phenomena, coining the term UFO (unidentified flying object) in the early 1950s because far from all unexplained objects in the sky were saucer shaped. All manner of newspaper and magazine articles and books came out as interest in the subject continued to grow; thus, the seed for spotting, researching and documenting UFOs was sown around the world and continues to grow to this day.

This book recounts just the tip of the iceberg of reported UFO sightings over Britain from the last 115 years. Drawing on a huge array of newspapers, magazines, books, scrapbooks and interviews I have collected, as well as archives and private collections I have had privileged access to for my research over the past thirty years, I have selected some the most notable and intriguing as well as some of the lesser-known sightings from across Britain, from the 'scareships' of 1909, mysterious lights, orbs and 'Foo Fighters' during the Second World War to the Rendlesham Incident in December 1980 (Britain's Roswell) and the Dudley Dorito of the 2010s.

The stream of sightings does not appear to be drying up either. Since 2021 over 1,000 UFO sightings have been recorded over the UK. According to the UFO Identified website, just under half (some 48 per cent) of all reported UFO sightings over recent years come with photographic, phone camera or film evidence. The most common shape of the reported UFOs during this period is a star (25 per cent), followed by orbs (17 per cent), spheres (10 per cent) and cylinders (9 per cent), but of course other forms are also seen.

Every story in this book was recorded and often published in newspapers, magazines and specialist journals as a truthful account of a UFO incident. These cases were witnessed by a huge variety of credible witnesses including members of the military services, ex-military, police and people of many ages from all walks of life. I have tried to publish the earliest and purest accounts given personally by the witnesses to the incidents. I do mention some of the official explanations, retractions and denials regarding what may or may not have been seen, but I try not to get embroiled in conspiracy theories. I leave you, the reader, to make your own minds up about the stories that follow.

The truth is out there.

Neil R. Storey
Norwich

Chapter 1

A New Century

Scareships Over East Anglia 1909

Between March and May 1909 newspapers across Britain carried accounts of 'mystery airships' that were seen and heard traversing the night sky over East Anglia and Wales. To put this into some context, the Wright brothers had only achieved the first powered flight six years prior in 1903, Bleriot would not fly across the Channel until 25 July 1909 and the first Channel crossings by airship would be over a year away.

Anglo-German relations had become strained after the Germans started building their own warships to rival the pride of the British fleet HMS *Dreadnought*. Furthermore, the distrust and perception of sinister anti-British machinations of the German nation had featured in the popular press, magazine part works and books for a number of years previously with such works as Erskine Childers' *Riddle of the Sands* (1903) and *The Invasion of 1910* (1906) and *Spies of the Kaiser* (1909) by the doyen of European alarmist fiction William le Queux ably demonstrating the tenor of such literature.

In the spring of 1909 newspapers were reporting the successful distance trials of Zeppelins in Germany. In the climate of anti-German fears, many considered the purpose of these monstrous creations was a sinister one and wondered how long it would be before they came over England. People in East Anglia, after centuries of watching the natural harbours along their coastline for raiders and invaders for centuries, were particularly on their guard.

Alleged spies and suspicious characters had already been reported at a number of locations. A year earlier, in 1908, the Secretary of State for

War had been asked in the House of Commons if he could say anything concerning 'a ride through England organised by a foreign power' and whether he had received any official information or reports from chief constables in the eastern counties as to espionage in England by foreign nations.

With all this as backdrop, early on the morning of 23 March 1909 PC James Kettle of the Peterborough Borough Police was patrolling his beat when his attention was caught by a strange sound and he spotted something extraordinary in the sky, so extraordinary he described exactly what he saw to a reporter from the *Peterborough Citizen and Advertiser*:

> I was on duty in Cromwell Road and was coming out of Cobden Street into that thoroughfare when I heard what I took to be a motor car, which I judged was some 400 yards distant. It was 5.15am, and still quite dark. I walked along Cromwell Road, expecting to see the lights of an approaching car, but none appeared. Still I could hear the steady buzz of a high-powered engine, and suddenly it struck me that the sound was coming, not along the surface of the road, but from above! I looked up, and my eye was at once attracted by a powerful light, which I should judge to have been some 1,200ft above the earth. Outlined against the stars was a dark body. The object was somewhat oblong and narrow in shape, outlined against the stars. It seemed to be about a couple of yards long [when viewed in the sky from the ground] and I am quite sure that there was no gas bag, as would have been the case in a dirigible balloon. When I first sighted the machine it was not straight overhead but appeared to be over the railway in the direction of Taverners Road. It was going at a tremendous pace, and as I watched, the rattle of the engines gradually grew fainter and fainter, and it disappeared into the north-west. Altogether I should say I saw it for about three minutes.

With that one incident, PC Joseph Kettle became the first member of a uniformed service to go on public record as a witness of a UFO in the twentieth century. What he saw reached the ears of the press and the subsequent reportage drew interest from numerous national and local newspapers. An interview with PC Kettle was also published in the *East Anglian Daily Times* on 26 March 1909, where Kettle began by explaining exactly what he had seen:

I saw almost above me an airship. It had a powerful light, and was a considerable distance from the earth. In fact, it looked little more than a couple of yards long.

Q. What shape was it?

A. Oblong. And it was travelling as fast as an express train. I could not, of course, see anyone in it, it was too dark.

Q. Couldn't it have been a balloon?

A. Oh, no. I heard the motor distinctly, and besides it was oblong in shape.

Q. Which way was it travelling?

A. It seemed as if it had come from the direction of Castor.

Q. And did it pass above you?

A. Yes, almost immediately above me. If it had been half an hour later I should have been able to see anyone inside it; it would have been light. When I first saw the machine it was not straight overhead, but a little to the west. It was going at a tremendous pace and as I watched the motor of the engines grew fainter and fainter and the machine disappeared into the north west…When Kettle's sergeant came up a short time afterwards he was told of the airship, but strange to say he had neither seen nor heard it.

Others came forward claiming they had also witnessed the object over Peterborough on that same night as PC Kettle's sighting. Miss Gill, the daughter of the city electrical engineer, was returning from the theatre with two friends. They saw a bright flashing light, apparently attached to 'some dark object, moving slowly in the direction of Cromwell Road. The whole thing happened very quickly, and I lost sight of it almost at once'.

Kettle's story was circulated in newspapers around the country and members of the public began to come forward from other areas relating their own accounts of what they had seen in the sky over Britain.

Authorities, perhaps even as lofty as those in government and Whitehall were no doubt concerned over the potential panic such accounts could create. Perhaps unsurprisingly, an unnamed police officer was put forward to speak to the members of the press to nip the situation in the bud by explaining Kettle had actually been 'mistaken'.

The whirring he had heard was attributed to the noise from the Co-operative Society bakery on Cobden Street and the object he had seen looming across the sky was dismissed as being a Chinese lantern attached to 'a very fine kite flying over the neighbourhood of Cobden', and the speed Kettle had stated it was travelling across the sky was brushed off as 'a little poetic touch for the benefit of your interviewers'. There was, however, no explanation offered as to why anyone should be flying a kite with a Chinese lantern attached at 5.15 a.m. Descendants of PC James Kettle recall he always swore that he was not mistaken and had seen an unidentified flying object. He would also not remain alone in sighting the strange object and hearing the strange sound that accompanied it in the sky over East Anglia during the spring of 1909.

Despite the repudiation of PC Kettle's statement, witnesses continued to come forward with more sightings. In mid-April, Mr F. Baxter came forward to the *Evening News* on 17 May with what he saw over the New England area of Peterborough:

> I was returning from the theatre where I play in the orchestra, about 10.50...when I saw a bright light in the sky. I said to my mate, 'What's that up there?' and he replied 'It's the moon'. No further notice was taken until we had gone about half a mile further, when we saw the light travelling very rapidly in a north westerly direction. Several other people noticed it. We ran to a large field, where we got a good view. We could make out a long black body, in the front of which was a very bright light, the shape of a fantail pigeon. I could not say at what speed it was going, but it was not many minutes before it passed out of sight.

Norfolk farm labourer Fred Harrison's sighting at Terrington Marsh on the night of 21 April 1909 was published in the *Daily Express*:

> I was outside New Common Marsh Farm about a quarter to ten at night when I saw the airship. I heard a whirring noise overhead, and when I looked up I saw the fields round were lit up by a bright light. I was startled and wondered whatever it could be. Then I saw the light

> came from a long, dark airship which was travelling swiftly overhead. It was low down – only a little way above the trees – so I could see it plainly. It seemed to be 80 or 100 feet long, and I could distinguish two men on a kind of hanging platform below. The searchlight lit up the road, the farm buildings, the trees and everything it touched, so that it was like day. I could even read the printing on some bills on the wall. The airship passed right over New Common Marsh Farm, and went in the direction of Hunstanton, on the other side of the Wash. It was travelling very fast against the wind, and it was out of sight in a few minutes.

At around 8 p.m. on 24 April 1909, PC Hudson was on duty in the vicinity of Gippeswyk Park in Ipswich, Suffolk, when his attention was drawn to a light in the sky: 'It appeared to be at a great height, and I lost sight of it at intervals. Whilst I was watching the light I suddenly observed a dark object which appeared to be about a hundred yards from the lighted one. I examined it through a pair of opera glasses and the dark object appeared to be like an ordinary balloon. After hovering about for a time it passed out of sight in a south westerly direction.'

Quite a crowd gathered to watch the object, and another witness, Mr J. A. Smith, said: 'It did not appear to be an aeroplane, but rather an elongated gas bag, with a car carrying lights at a considerable distance below ... Powerful lights were used at times, but I heard no sound.' The object was seen to move off against the wind.

Other sightings were reported over the ensuing weeks from locations across eastern England. Some people ventured the idea the airship was the secret invention of a British aeronaut who housed his flying machine in some remote farm building between Market Harborough and Peterborough, but more were of the opinion the airship was German in origin and, whatever its mission, it was ominous. In one notable instance on Friday 7 May, 'a long sausage dirigible balloon' was spotted over New Holland Gap, a mile and a half from Clacton-on-Sea in Essex.

On 9 May, Miss H. M. Boville of No. 13 Warrior Square, Southend, spotted another:

> I was closing the window of my bedroom which faces NE about 11.20pm, when I noticed a very large dark object looming out of the sky and travelling slowly from the direction of Shoeburyness. At first

> I thought it was the gunpowder cloud that one sees after an explosion, it was so opaque and black and the night was too dark to enable me to see it clearly. After a few seconds, however, it crossed the sky and remained nearly stationary in front of my window. I could see the outline of a torpedo-shaped airship, very long and large. It was not more than about a quarter of a mile above the houses and trees, and remained immovable for a few minutes, then rose higher and travelled very swiftly in a westerly direction towards the coast and London, showing as it did so, two very powerful searchlights at either end for a second or two. I did not hear any sound from the engines as it was too far off, nor could I discern the aeronauts but the vessel seemed to travel very steadily and smoothly.

The sightings kept coming. Mr C. W. Allen, the pedestrian holder of the 2,000 miles road record who lived in Market Harborough, was motoring through the local countryside with two friends:

> When passing through the village of Kelmarsh, Northamptonshire about seven miles from Market Harborough, we heard a loud report in the air, like the backfire of a motor car. Then we heard distinctly from above our heads the 'tock-tock-tock' of a swiftly running motor engine and we looked up. I was sitting on the front seat, next to the driver, and had a clear view of a dark shape looming up out of the night. It was an oblong airship, with lights in front and behind, flying swiftly through the air.
>
> It seemed some five or six hundred feet up and must have been at least 100 ft long. The lights were not very bright but we could distinctly see the torpedo shape and what appeared to be men on the platform below. The steady buzz of the engines could be heard through the still air and we watched it until it passed out of sight in a north easterly direction towards Peterborough. It was travelling at least twenty miles an hour, easily and steadily, and appeared to be answering the helm like a ship. I cannot doubt the evidence of my senses, and my two companions, both practical men, are convinced that the Peterborough district contains the home of the airship.

At about 1.20 a.m. on Saturday 15 May, Mrs Fricker of Victoria Road, Great Yarmouth, was engaged in her duties as night nurse to a Mrs H. Lawrence when she noticed what she described as 'a balloon-shaped object on the west side of the destructor on Caister Road. First it showed brilliant white, then a pale greenish light and next a reddish one.' All in all, she observed the object in the sky for about an hour and then looked away as she tried to go about her business. When she looked again it was gone.

On Sunday 16 May, Mr Edwards, chief clerk from Lowestoft solicitor Seth Bailey, had missed his last train home. It was shortly after midnight and he was about a quarter of a mile outside North Walsham, Norfolk when he witnessed a 'scareship':

> ...something attracted my attention, and upon looking round and lifting my eyes over a fence I saw two or three lights and they appeared to be a short distance from the ground. I paid very little heed to them and walked on. However, I had walked a few hundred yards when I again heard a peculiar noise and this time looked around, I noticed a glaring light, and it seemed to be coming towards me. To make certain that there was something moving I got behind a large tree. I got into a position so that the light was entirely obliterated from my sight, and then I observed a dark object ascending. It passed over my head and proceeded in the direction of Yarmouth and Lowestoft.

North Lowestoft resident Mrs Wigg was awakened at 1.30 a.m. by a noise similar to that of a motor car. Looking through the window directly opposite her bed, she saw a dark object pass quickly heading south-west. It was not very high and was bottle shaped, in a horizontal position and of considerable length; she saw what appeared to be a man steering at the front of the machine. Several other people saw vivid flashes or heard engine sounds at that time. Mr T. Plowman, who resided in the same house, added that at the same time he was in the next room and was dazzled by a brilliant light, which appeared to be a searchlight.

Mrs Edith Sterry (wife of coal merchant Herbert Steward Sterry) of North Parade, Lowestoft, also saw a powerful light pass her window on Sunday night. All of these witnesses were local people, so when it was suggested they were simply mistaken and were actually seeing the beam of the lighthouse they would be entitled to feel their claims were being dismissed out of hand.

On at 7.45 a.m. on Sunday 16 May, Captain Gerald Hervey, the Local Government Board Inspector for the Eastern District, stated he was at Brome, near Eye, on the Norfolk and Suffolk border where he observed 'a cigar-shaped balloon sailing towards Lowestoft and a height of about a quarter of a mile and three or four miles distant. The airship was travelling in an easterly direction, a little south of Lowestoft and therefore going against the wind.'

Concerns over these incidents and the ensuing press coverage of the 'mystery airships' led to questions being asked by local MPs in the House of Commons on 17 May 1909. Sir Arthur Fell, MP for Great Yarmouth, directed a question to Richard Haldane, the Secretary of State for War, enquiring what were the number of dirigibles both constructed and under construction by Germany. Haldane replied that seven airships had been built and another five were under construction. However, when Horatio Myer, MP for Lambeth North, enquired: 'Will the honourable gentleman, in any report he may circulate, tell us about a certain dirigible supposed to be hovering over our coast?' The question was greeted with laughter and no reply was given. That same night, between 8.30 and 9 p.m., George Burwood, the skipper of the Lowestoft trawler *Red Rose*, was about 6 miles off Southwold when he saw what he described as 'a balloon high up in the air'. He observed it carried no visible lights and was running before the wind in the direction of Ostend. The aerial phenomena was also observed by a number of Norfolk and Suffolk coastguards who were on duty that night.

Further concerns were raised after reports were received of 'strange manoeuvres' in the North Sea by the German Navy. It was even suggested in press reports that the mystery airships now being seen over the eastern counties might have been launched from German battleships to perform night time spying missions over Britain. In May, Captain Egenes of the Norwegian steamer *St Olaf* which traded between Blyth, Northumberland and Sarpsborg, Norway, reported that at night when the vessel was only a short distance from the British side a large airship carrying five searchlights suddenly appeared and hovered directly above the vessel and directed all its lights in the steamer's bridge. The airship was within hailing distance but gave no answer to the challenge and owing to the blinding glare of the searchlights it was difficult to distinguish any details. Suddenly the airship swung off after another steamer a mile or so away, on which also the searchlights were directed. The airship afterwards made off at a sharp rate towards the south and seemed to scrutinise another steamer a short distance away in the same manner.

Such reports appearing in the press brought forward Skipper James Henry Stockman of Lowestoft, owner of the fishing smack *Superb* who related an incident he had experienced when on the North Sea, 33–35 miles north-east of Lowestoft, on one clear starlight night in October 1908. He suddenly saw what at first appeared to be a large star rising out of the water and travelling towards the vessel. He was struck by the unusual sight and called up one of his crew to look at it.

It occurred to him that he could show a red flare and try to discover what the object might be. He lit the flare and, much to his surprise, the airship answered his signal with a red flare. Skipper Stockman next lit a white flare and received a second response with a blue flare. The wind was west or west-north-west and the object was travelling almost with the wind a little on its quarter in an east-north-east direction. He kept the object in view for twenty to thirty minutes when it sailed away seawards. Mr Stockman said he saw only one light on the airship and was sure that it was not a balloon because when its flare was burning he observed that its outline was sausage shaped.

Further analysis of the situation was offered in a measured report by the Berlin correspondent of the *Daily Express* on 14 May 1909:

> It is admitted by German experts that the mysterious airship which has been seen hovering over the east coast of England may be a German airship. England possesses no such airship and no French airship has hitherto sailed so far as the distance from Calais to Peterborough. On the other hand, the performance of several German airships, including the Gross airship, which has made one voyage of thirteen hours, would render it possible for them to reach the English coast. At the same time it is improbable that the German airship seen above England ascended from German soil. An aerial voyage to the English coast would still be a dangerous and formidable undertaking even for the newest airships.

By the time the *Daily Express* article was published, however, sightings of mystery airships had been reported over Ely, St Neots, Wisbech, Peakirk, Orton and Wingland in Cambridgeshire; and from Ipswich, Saxmundham, Bradfield St George and Woolpit in Suffolk and Southend-on-Sea in Essex. There was even a report that a mystery airship had been spotted by servants over the king's estate at Sandringham in Norfolk.

Witnesses generally agreed the object they had seen in the sky was cigar shaped, was at least 100 feet in length, the engines had made a throbbing noise and it appeared to perform its manoeuvres at a steady pace and with ease. The reports often mentioned some beam of light or 'searchlight' had shone down from the craft onto land and structures below it.

At dusk on Wednesday 19 May 1909 a mystery 'airship' was spotted at great altitude over Shoeburyness by a Royal Artillery sergeant. On that same night possibly one of the very first instances of a UFO affecting vehicles in their proximity happened to a man who would only be described in the press as 'a well-known gentleman' who resided in the Broadland village of Wroxham. He was riding his motorbike homeward over Wroxham Bridge when his lamp suddenly went out. Stopping his motorbike to dismount and investigate what the problem was, the witness was suddenly hit by a powerful beam of light from the sky directly above him. Dazzled by the light, he could not see nor hear any airship. Upon arrival home he told his story to his brother, who said that while he was at the Norwich suburb village of Sprowston (about 5 miles from Wroxham) he had also seen 'a strangle light in the sky but could not see from whence it came.'

A short time later a number of residents of the New Catton, the Norwich suburb which adjoins Sprowston, spotted bright lights in the sky. Mrs Turner of Traverse Street, Waterloo Road, was returning from the theatre at around 11.30 p.m.:

> As I came into my street, a flash of light came on me all of a sudden and made the street look like day. I was by myself but there were two young people in the street – a youth standing near his bicycle and next to a young lady. I heard one of them say 'What's that?' I could hear a noise like the whizzing of wheels. I looked up and there I saw a big star of light in front and a big searchlight behind. I saw no body of an airship. I only saw the light and heard the noise. It was coming from North-North-East from the direction of Angel Road School and flying very low, so low that it would have touched the pinnacle of the school had it passed directly over it.

A torpedo-shaped object with what was thought to be a powerful searchlight was also observed by a Mr Chatten, a young grocer's assistant, as he rode his bicycle through Tharston around midnight. Just after he passed the residence of Mr Berney Ficklin:

> I was dazzled by a bright light shining from right above me. The trees and hedges were lit up brilliantly. I have seen a naval searchlight at Harwich and I should suppose that what I saw was something of that sort, but there was a bluish tinge about it and it did not appear to me as strong as the naval lights. It seemed to be off again after only a few seconds. Getting off my bicycle and looking upwards, the tapering end going foremost ... and was moving rapidly in the direction of Norwich. On the underside was what I should call an iron bar, supporting a sort of framework, a yellow light shining at each end. I could not see any men upon the framework, nor could I hear any buzzing sound as a motor would cause but this is not to be wondered at because although the night was still, the thing was travelling at great height. The sky was rather dark, but there was light enough for me to see the airship plainly outlined against it. I do not speak with any misgiving on the subject. I am confident about what I saw.

Scareships Over Wales

As the eastern counties of England were abuzz with accounts of scareships, similar sightings began to occur over the west of Britain in Wales. One of the first recorded sightings occurred on 16 May 1909 when Oliver L. Jones of the well-known local auctioneers Messrs Nelmes, Pole, Jackson and Jones was driving with his wife and two friends from Tregarog to Monmouth at 10.30 p.m.:

> It was about eight miles from Monmouth when I first saw it. It came from the direction of Usk and Raglan, and seemed to go towards Chepstow. It then turned right round and came back towards Raglan and over the mountain. I continued to drive slowly on and watched it for half an hour, but the airship seemed to go faster than that. It went up and down and around in a remarkable manner. There were lights in front and behind, and they seemed to be about 15 yards apart. I could see the cigar shape quite distinctly, and noticed the perfect control the occupants had over the airship. There were four lights in front and one behind. Mr Jones's brother was also driving in the area and also saw the object.

Just two days later a strange encounter worthy of the pen of Jules Verne happened to Mr Charles Lethbridge, a travelling showman of Roland Street, Newtown, Cardiff, who was crossing the Caerphilly Mountain on foot with his Punch and Judy show late on the night of Tuesday 18 May 1909:

> I work during the winter months at the Cardiff docks but in the summertime I travel the district as a showman, giving performances at the various schools. Yesterday I went to Senghenydd and proceeded to walk home over Caerphilly Mountain. You know that the top of that mountain is a very lonely spot. I reached it about 11.00pm and when turning the bend at the summit I saw a long tube-shaped affair lying on the grass with two men close to it. They attracted my attention because of their peculiar get-up – big heavy fur coats and fur caps fitting tightly over their heads.
>
> The noise of my little spring cart seemed to attract them and when they saw me they they jumped up and jabbered furiously to each other in a strange lingo. When I was twenty yards away from them they hurriedly collected something from the ground and then I was really frightened. The long thing on the ground rose up slowly. I was standing still at the time, quite amazed and when it was hanging a few feet off the ground the men jumped into a kind of little carriage suspended from it, and gradually the whole affair and the men rose in the air in a zig-zag fashion.
>
> When they had cleared the telegraph wires that pass over the mountain, two lights like electric lamps shone out and then went higher into the air and sailed away towards Cardiff. I was too frightened to move for a time but I pulled myself together and as soon as I came home told my people about what I had seen.

Just two hours after Lethbridge's encounter, according to an official statement made to the Cardiff Docks Company by Signalman Robert Westlake at 1.15 a.m. on Wednesday 19 May:

> While attending to my duty signalling trains at King's Junction of the Queen Alexandra Dock, I was startled by a weird object flying in the air. In appearance it represented a boat of cigar shape making a whizzing noise. It was lit up by two lights, which could be plainly seen. It was travelling at a great rate and was elevated at a distance of half a mile, making for the eastward.
>
> There were many men working at the time loading the SS *Arndale* and the airship was seen by most of them. Five workmen, as well as the third mate of the *Arndale*, all testified to the facts recorded

> above. The airship came from the direction of Newport, took a curve over the docks and passed over the channel towards Weston being clearly in view for a minute or two until its lights were suddenly extinguished. Several other night workmen who were interviewed corroborated the story.

On the evening of Wednesday 19 May a mysterious airship was also seen over Pontypool by a number of people on the streets, Post Office officials and workmen. Local architect Mr Gath Fisher and his wife both saw the object in the sky. Mr Fisher described what he saw as 'cigar shaped ... there was a powerful light at each end'. Men on night duty at Pontypool town forge declared that the 'airship' floated over them and then darted off in the direction of Herefordshire.

Three days later, at 10.30 p.m. on Saturday 22 May, Maesteg's Commerical Street was crowded with miners and their wives shopping when people began noticing the lights of an airship that appeared to be hovering above the town. Some said the lights were extinguished after a few moments and others said that they travelled slowly over Garwen Mountain. One man went so far as to declare that he clearly made out the flying machine through a telescope and could even see people on board it.

Meanwhile, on the evening of 22 May at Aberystwyth, Cardigan Bay, fourteen witnesses saw bright lights burst into view like an electric lamp. The lights were travelling in from the sea, heading south-east. Published accounts stated: 'At one point ... the lower light was flashed on to the sea and it looked very much like a searchlight. The lights hovered two miles offshore, then moved towards the pier-head and disappeared.' The lights were so bright that at first the witnesses thought it was moonlight. Upon seeing the lights in the sky, a Great Western Railway guard at once exclaimed, 'It's the airship.' Those who witnessed the lights were left with the impression they appeared to be searching the bay.

Scareship lights appeared over Swansea on Monday 24 May 1909. PC Williams of the Swansea Police Force made an official report that at about midnight he distinctly saw, from Port Tennant, an airship going in a north-westerly direction at great speed and with a powerful light. The constable reported that a man named Bell called his attention to a light moving in the air, and after a while an airship was spotted passing along in a north-westerly direction at great speed. The light attached to the airship was located under it and was exceedingly bright. The airship was at such a height that it was impossible for the observer to obtain a good description of it, and eventually it passed out of sight. PC Johnston says he saw a 'bright moving light', but he would not swear it was an airship.

Scareship Over the Tyne

Retrospective accounts of the mystery airships rightly place the 1909 sightings around the eastern counties between the months of March and May, with another series of sightings occurring in Wales during May. However, one of the least known, yet most compelling, sightings of the scareships occurred in the north-east of Britain in early June 1909.

Master Stevedore Alexander Mitchell (at the time a member of Tynemouth Town Council; he was made Mayor of Tynemouth in 1921) was supervising his working gang of men who were employed loading the steamer *Harford* that was lying in Tyne Dock, South Shields, in Tyne and Wear. At around 11 p.m. Mr Mitchell's attention was attracted by a peculiar reflection in the water. Looking skyward, he discerned the large shape in the sky immediately overhead that was causing it. With the aid of powerful binoculars, he made out an oblong object of great size which was apparently carrying a powerful searchlight. All of his workmen saw it too; at first they thought it was a reflection, but closer examination through the binoculars satisfied them that it was 'an airship'.

For about an hour Mitchell and his men suspended work to watch its movements. He described the light as having been 'manipulated at intervals, the rays sometimes lighting up almost the whole expanse of Jarrow Slake. At times the object would be motionless and at others it would dart in different directions.' Finally, it made a complete circuit of the Slake and then moved away over the course of the Tyne, proceeding down the river towards the harbour's mouth, where it was lost from sight around midnight. Newspaper reports also pointed out that Mr Mitchell's account of what he and his men witnessed was independently borne out by his men when questioned by reporters.

It was later claimed in the press, without any attribution to the source of the information, that what Councillor Mitchell and his men had seen was an airship that was 'an invention of a Tyneside firm out on experimental flight'. The problem with that claim is that no Tyneside firm has so far been traced that was making airships or any other lighter-than-air aircraft at that time. Indeed, it would be months later that the first recorded powered flight would took place in Northumberland when Mr George William Parkinson of Gosforth made a successful flight in his Bleriot monoplane at Wideopen in November 1909.

Winston Churchill is known to have taken a personal interest in the scareships and the fear they caused among the British population. This undoubtedly sowed seeds in his mind that would spur him on to press for the Air Navigation Act when he was Secretary of State for the Home Department in 1911, during the debate of which he stated: '...there is a certain danger to be guarded against not so much from aeroplanes falling upon crowds, but from the possibility of panic through the idea or even the cry of aeroplanes or other aerial machines passing over the heads of a great crowd. One great danger always is to get a big crowd in motion.'

Churchill acted swiftly again when he was First Lord of the Admiralty when an unidentified aircraft was spotted over the Royal Navy torpedo school at Sheerness in Essex in October 1912 and he ordered an investigation to be made to establish the identity and origin of the craft. No successful identification was made, but the climate of fear and suspicion being what it was as the storm clouds of the First World War were gathering, it was assumed the Germans were behind it.

It is also interesting to note that it was in the wake of the scares and suspicions of the scareships that both the Security Service (MI5), responsible for homeland security, and the Secret Intelligence Service (SIS or MI6), Britain's foreign intelligence service, began operations as a single organisation known as the Secret Service Bureau in October 1909.

After decades of research, neither the author of this book nor any other British nor international historian to date (and there are many who have spent decades focusing solely on Zeppelin air raids) have uncovered a single official document or even a memoir by a Zeppelin commander or member of aircrew that offers any evidence or claim that Zeppelins flew over Britain in 1909.

Strange Craft Over the Northumberland Coast

In the years before the establishment of the nomenclature of UFOs in the 1950s, what to call mysterious objects spotted in the sky remained something of a quandary for the British press, who often resorted to such terms as 'mystery airship' or 'aircraft', such as this account from the Northumberland coast in 1913:

> A Sunderland correspondent telegraphs: About eight o'clock yesterday morning an aircraft was observed from Sunderland to fall into the sea whilst flying about three miles off the land. It remained visible for a few

minutes, and then disappeared. There was a rough sea on at the time, and it is feared that the airman has been drowned. Nothing has yet been picked up connected with the machine, which, when it fell, was flying in a southerly direction.

With reference to the above, a Blyth correspondent says: An airship or aeroplane was observed seawards off Church Point, Newbiggin, on the Northumberland coast, about three o'clock yesterday morning. The aircraft came from a southerly direction. At intervals red, green, and white lights were shown. Presently, as if in response to signals, a steamer came from a northerly direction and anchored just north of Church Point. Soon afterwards both steamer and aircraft proceeded in a southerly direction, being speedily lost to view. The mysterious movements of the unknown steamer and aircraft were kept under observation from the shore, but darkness precluded identification of either vessel.

Chapter 2

Two World Wars

A 1914 Scareship

The First World War broke out on 4 August 1914, and little more than two months later, on 20 October 1914, before Britain had been shelled from Imperial German Navy cruisers off the coast and before a bomb had been dropped by aircraft or Zeppelin, a UFO drew widespread curiosity from local people as it hovered over the port of Blyth in Northumberland. *The Illustrated Chronicle* of Wednesday 21 October 1914 reported:

> It [the mystery airship] was first seen shortly after 8.00pm and for nearly three quarters of an hour lights were exhibited at intervals of three to ten minutes. Almost the entire population of the town turned into the streets to see what they could of the mysterious visitor and the general opinion was that the light was being carried by some type of aircraft.
>
> The night was dark, with only a few stars visible, and the flying machine was far too high to enable one to ascertain whether it was of the aeroplane or airship type. One thing however, was certain, it hung about the vicinity of the town for over half an hour and apparently manoeuvred in a circle. People were curious and strained their eyes and craned their necks in endeavours to elucidate the mystery, while many cracked jokes regarding the threatened Zeppelin raid from Germany. Eventually the light disappeared as strangely as it came and the town soon assumed its normal conditions. Subsequent enquiries in official quarters went to show that the visit of the mysterious aircraft was totally unexpected and there was a disposition to view the circumstance as being suspicious.

Mystery Lights and Zeppelin Raiders

The first Zeppelin air raid to be carried out on Britain took place on the evening of 19 January 1915. Three Zeppelins set out but only two, the L3 and the L4, made landfall over the Norfolk coast near Bacton. The L3, under the command of Kapitänleutnant Hans Fritz, found its way to Great Yarmouth where it dropped bombs and claimed the first two air-raid victims of the war; the L4, under Kapitänleutnant Count Magnus von Platen Hallermund, made landfall near Bacton then turned to the west of the county, claiming two lives and wounding many others at King's Lynn.

There was talk of the Zeppelins using searchlights to find the locations they wished to bomb. German artists of the Zeppelin raid on England played up to this belief, depicting Zeppelins shining lights on postcards and in magazines, but the simple fact is that Zeppelins were not actually fitted with searchlights. To ascertain what was below them at night, Zeppelin crew would drop flares.

Holcombe Ingleby, the Member of Parliament for King's Lynn, was particularly concerned that the reports he received from reliable local people of powerful lights being shone out in West Norfolk were being ignored by authorities. He raised the matter in Parliament and produced what is now a rare and collectable booklet, *The Zeppelin Raid in West Norfolk* (1915). In its pages a number of named witnesses go on record with their accounts of the lights they saw before and during the air raid.

Geoffrey Girling, William Playford and Mr Patchett (a farmer who lived at Heacham Bottom) among others independently reported lights that were assumed to have been shone from a car but were more powerful than any car headlamps. They were observed shining out from the area of Snettisham Hill near Heacham a week *before* the raid, and during it. Girling recalled the lights were 'flashing upwards, that seemed to be flashing out to sea and that on being observed the car moved to another point on the same road, from which it also flashed. The light was very bright and more like a searchlight than a motor-car lamp.'

Some believed they saw a car, while others were far more taken by moving lights they assumed to be a car. Miss Mitchell and her brother resided in the last house in Burnham Deepdale. Their attention was caught by an 'unusually powerful light' at 10 p.m. on the night of the air raid: 'Although the night was dark, the road narrow, and the light dim, it travelled at a faster rather rate than Miss Mitchell had ever observed.'

A 'brilliantly lighted motor car' was also seen by Miss Bethel and her servant in Heacham. She claimed a member of the locally based yeomanry even called out for them to put out their lights, but as it passed she claimed she saw it had 'three rows of seats, the first two occupied by four persons with strange muffled headgear. The car was so silent that its motion was inaudible.'

One Mr Sayer added he had been cycling along and was preparing to descend the hill leading to Heacham Bottom when he saw 'the sky was lit up by what I took to be a searchlight being worked from Hunstanton but which a few moments later proved to be a motor car carrying a very brilliant lamp on the top of the bonnet and proceeding towards Snettisham'. Mr H. C. Sheringham, a well-known local farmer, lived on high ground and claimed he had personally witnessed 'bright flashes sent upwards at six different points of the Zeppelin's journey'.

Witness accounts across West Norfolk, from Tuddenham Corner to Hunstanton, led Ingleby to conclude there were at least two cars in the area that were shining their brilliant lights, but no cars, collaborators or spies with powerful searchlights were ever discovered.

Were all of these reports purely paranoia? Could all the powerful beams of light that were seen have an earthly explanation? Or could some of them have been extraterrestrial – before a time when the term 'UFO' existed and the notion of alien life was firmly believed by most people to only exist in the realms of science-fiction books? Similar sightings of mysterious lights would recur during the Second World War.

Flying Platform Over Aldeburgh

Mr A. E. Whiteland of Saxmundham, Suffolk, sent this remarkable account to Gordon Creighton which was reproduced in *Flying Saucer News* in 1968. Mr Whiteland tells of how his mother often retold the story of how when she had been a young girl living in Aldeburgh, Suffolk, during the First World War she saw a UFO pass by. It was 1916/17 and she had been looking out of an upstairs window just before lunch on a bright, sunny day when she saw, coming off the nearby marshes at a little above the level of her house, a round platform with a hollow centre and what appeared to be two brass handrails. Holding tightly onto this rail were around twelve men, standing shoulder to shoulder and wearing blue uniforms and round hats like sailors pulled well down onto their heads. Each of the men appeared to have human features and were staring straight ahead.

This strange 'platform' had no obvious engine, wings or airship above it from which it was suspended. It came straight along the road of terraced houses where she lived, travelling 'as fast as a man can run' until it was within 100 yards of her house, then suddenly turned away at a right angle from her and went between the Railway Hotel and the shed on the railway yard in the direction of the sea. The whole sighting lasted around five minutes.

Burton Dassett 'Ghost Lights', 1923

Many people continued to watch the skies in the years of peace that followed and seemed more confident reporting unexplained objects if they saw them. In December 1922, a 'spectral light' of a bluish tint that swooped through the air, assuming fantastic shapes as it did so, began to be seen in the countryside around Burton Dassett, Northend and Fenny Compton in south Warwickshire

The local people who encountered it declared their experience as 'nerve-racking'. The *Banbury Guardian* on 23 February 1923 reported:

> George White of Fennv Compton, who sallied out with field glasses and two companions, and who declares he not only saw the light, but that both his companions felt it pass over them. It was, he says, of a reddy-blue and creepy complexion. Harold Cotterill, a youth, returning from an errand at Northend saw it hovering round a lonely pool and the horse he was driving also saw it and was so startled that he had difficulty in controlling it. Other residents, who may be relied on not to be misled an imaginary ghost-story, also declare that they have seen it, so the appearance may be assumed to be based on reality.

A reporter from the *Birmingham Daily Gazette* visited to see for himself and even chased the mysterious light with locals on consecutive nights armed with torches. The reporter described what he saw as 'a well defined light, spherical in shape and without radiations. It is brighter than any bicycle lamp and glows with a dull yellow colour, tinged when seen near at hand, with red. To liken it to a Chinese lantern describes it exactly'. Whatever it was it still eluded capture and defied explanation, other than it was some kind of 'Jenny burn tail' or will-o'-the-wisp.

Mystery Lights: UFOs or the Fifth Column?

One of the regular reported concerns during the early years of the Second World War was that of supposed Fifth Columnists shining lights and flashing signals – to whom it is unclear, as at this time mainland

Britain was not experiencing air raids. These incidents were reported to police and military authorities and thousands of man hours were expended on the investigations of each apparently credible sighting. As early as 28 November 1939, Guy Liddell of MI5's B Division, which was responsible for counterespionage in Britain, recorded in his diary how concerns were being raised 'about the large numbers of reports coming in, particularly from the Air Ministry, to the effect that lights have been seen flashing at various parts of the country'.

MI5 regional security liaison officers were drawn into a number of the investigations into these lights. The Birmingham region attempted to plot the approximate locations of the lights reported to see if their source could be tracked down and attributed to causes such as flares or very bright lights shot up by our own forces. There were other issues highlighted by a Merseyside chief constable: 'The difficulty as far as the police are concerned does not arise at all from the fact that lights are used for signalling purposes. The difficulty arises from the fact that during an air raid the sky is lit up by many different types of lights. There is no doubt that the vast majority of these lights are caused by Anti-Aircraft guns.'

But did this explanation really cover every possibility? With so many people, both civilians and military, watching the skies over Britain, many things were reported that in later years, when such matters were better understood, would be described as UFOs. In the days when early radar (AMES Type 1) could only pick up aircraft over the sea, the Observer Corps (made Royal Observer Corps in 1941) filled the gap with their posts of observers armed with binoculars, Micklethwait height corrector (otherwise known as the 'Post Instrument') and telephone lines to report overland sightings. Unknowns were unusual but specific orders stipulated that observers were to report an unidentified flying object under the code name of 'Pheno' and give the time, bearing and estimate of height.

Wartime 'Pheno' reports are known to have been made from all over the country, but sadly very few of these records seem to have survived. However, a series of incidents along the River Tyne certainly caught the attention of military authorities. The River Tyne was second only to the River Clyde as a shipbuilding area, so its anti-aircraft defences had to be robust. Predominantly, these consisted of anti-aircraft guns, 'Z Batteries' that fired UP (Unrotated Projectile) rockets, barrage balloons and fighter support.

There were numerous attempts made by the Luftwaffe to breach the Tyne defences, and it was during these raids that strange glowing white orbs estimated to be around the size of an Austin Seven car were being seen diving around in the sky above. Barrage balloon crews (many of whom were women) were particularly disturbed to see these orbs fly though the woven wire ropes that were fixed to the balloons and allowed them to rise and descend via a winch lorry. When elevated, the wire rope also made a dangerous obstacle in the air for any aircraft that might come into contact with it, let alone the barrage balloon itself.

So, what were the glowing white orbs that tore through these wire ropes and set the barrage balloon adrift? Crews examined the ropes and found that the ends of the rope 'cut' by the orbs, instead of a fray or clean cut, had been melted or 'cauterised'. Samples were sent to the Air Ministry, but no explanation was forthcoming other than the verbal suggestion from a visiting wing commander to the Tyne barrage balloon sites that what they had witnessed had been 'some sort of secret weapon' and in the interests of security they should not say anything more about what they had witnessed.

Abducted by Aliens, Cresswell, Northumberland, 1942

In September 1942, Albert Lancashire (twenty-seven) was on guard duty at Cresswell radar station, a Chain Home Low radar site on the Northumberland coast, not far from Newbiggin-by-the-Sea. It was a cold, dark night and Albert was at his post in front of a sentry box about 30 yards from the sea. Suddenly a light shone from the sky about 300 feet above and away from him over the sea. It was surrounded by a 'black cloud' and his immediate thought was 'What have the Germans invented now?' He went quickly into his box to try to see the object without being seen. The light, which was of a yellow colour, 'rolled back on itself' rather than being switched off, its position then being much lower with the object close to him but still over the water. Suddenly he felt compelled to go outside, and another light shone out a yard or so in front of him a little above his head. Startled, things then happened quickly: he either put down or dropped his rifle with a fixed bayonet, threw up his arms and felt himself drawn towards it, experienced a floating sensation, then blacked out.

Albert came round again a few minutes later a few yards away from where he blacked out. Shocked, dazed and disorientated, he lay on the ground for five or ten minutes as he regained his senses and tried to understand what had just happened to him; he was convinced that what he had encountered was something that was not of this world. Although he had been badly shaken by what he had experienced, he pulled himself together, carried on with his duties as sentry and did not report the matter. Over the months and years afterwards, however, Albert experienced a series of dreams or subconscious memories while in a dream-like state.

He recalled walking 'along the beam' from the spacecraft and being seized by pygmy-sized men and carried aboard a spacecraft. Once aboard, he recalls looking out of a large window and looking down at the sea. He saw the crew were the size of average humans and the captain had dark hair and was wearing goggles. Albert recalled being made to lay down on an examination table, looking upwards at the blue dome of the ceiling of the craft. He could see a man leaning over another long table construction and wearing a skull cap like a surgeon. He also wore very thick glasses or goggles and smiled as though in welcome. Albert was sure some sort of medical examination was carried out on him, but he could not remember details. He was, however, left with a persistent rash on his tongue for years afterwards.

The Glowing Cross in the Sky

During the First World War when there were particularly heavy losses in battles such as the Somme in 1916 and Passchendaele in 1917, there are stories of glowing crosses appearing in the sky over city areas in Britain where many men had been recruited from and had been killed in the war. Similar manifestations are claimed to have occurred during the Second World War over bombed areas where there had been particularly heavy civilian casualties. One of the best-attested visions of a glowing cross in the sky was seen over Ipswich during an air-raid alert on 27 April 1944, which was claimed to have been witnessed by hundreds. Moved by the story, Revd Harold Godfrey Green, rector of St Nicholas' Church in Ipswich, made his own inquiries and 'completely satisfied himself of the authenticity of the vision'. As a result, hundreds came to see if the cross would show itself again. The *Daily News* of 15 May 1944 reported: 'An hour-and-a-half before the service started people began to arrive from outlying villages. The authorities had to deal with telephone inquiries from all parts of the country from people who wanted to attend, for Ipswich is in a prohibited area. Nine hundred people packed into the church, which seats 500. They sat in the aisles and chancel and in the tower. Two rows stood before the choir stalls. The vicar's sermon was relayed to the crowd outside through a loud-speaker system.'

Sadly, the vision did not make another appearance, but this would not be the last we would hear of glowing crosses...

Gremlins, Death Rays and Foo Fighters 1940–45

From early in the Second World War RAF pilots began blaming any problems with their aircraft, their cockpit instruments or radios on 'gremlins'. This possibly began as a throw-away term, but as the war progressed some pilots began to claim they had actually seen the mischievous little creatures with their own eyes. Roald Dahl, author of children's books such as *Charlie and the Chocolate Factory* and *The BFG*, was a fighter pilot during the war and produced a book for Walt Disney about these 'gremlins'. An animated film was even planned about them, but it did not come to fruition. Other cartoon books were created about gremlins, but whether they were just figments of the imagination or if there was something more to it was never fully proved either way.

Another strange wartime phenomena was that of a suspected 'death ray', which the Germans were thought to have developed, that brought down numerous Allied aircraft during raids on enemy territory. The problem emerged after the war when the Germans asked the Allied air force leaders to reveal the 'death ray' *they* thought *we* had developed that had brought down so many of their aircraft. Was this really down to the haste on both sides to mass produce fighter and bomber aircraft, causing so many of them appear to just 'fall out of the air'? Or, as some pilots and aircrew would wonder, was there another intelligent force involved that belonged to neither side that brought the aircraft down?

UFO Crash in Britain, 1945

The technological advances in aerial warfare during the Second World War were truly unprecedented by any war in history. The development of ever more advanced aircraft and rockets was cloaked in secrecy by each belligerent power and there were stories circulating of terrifying new weaponry through rumour, tall tales and black propaganda. In the years after the end of the conflict in 1945, many who had served were still bound under the Official Secrets Act to remain silent about what they had seen or what intelligence they had been privy to.

Long after the carnage of the war in the air had ended, a rumour persisted that something very out of the ordinary had crash-landed in Britain (or at least had landed under the control of British forces) during the closing months of the war in 1945 and was being examined by British scientists. After checking the experimental craft and development sites captured after the fall of Nazi Germany and the known Russian developments (so the story goes, at least), the recovered wreckage proved to be unidentifiable from any known earthly technology.

In 1955, when the debate was over, Air Ministry announced that a five-year probe by the Royal Air Force had been submitted as a report to senior officers, but the findings were never revealed to the public for security reasons. In the wake of the announcement, the pressure was on from the press and many other interested parties to at least discover if the inquiry concluded if flying saucers existed or not. All that could be ascertained was an implied denial of their existence. When a question was asked in Parliament of George Ward, the Under Secretary of State for Air, he confirmed reports of UFOs were investigated as they came in but denied there had been any formal inquiry.

At a time when the debate over the existence of UFOs was very much a hot topic, Dorothy Kilgallen, a respected American columnist and investigative reporter on the *New York Journal-American*, was on holiday in Britain with her husband, the Broadway producer and radio commentator Dick Kollmar. Kilgallen, best known to American audiences as a regular panellist on the television game show *What's My Line?*, cabled this remarkable story through the London office of the International News Service of a crashed alien spacecraft that came into Allied hands in the late stages of the Second Word War, which would appear in a number of newspapers across America and around the world:

> London, May 22 – I can report today on a story which is positively spooky, not to mention chilling. British Scientists and airmen, after examining the wreckage of one mysterious flying ship, are convinced these strange aerial objects are not optical illusions or Soviet inventions, but are flying saucers which originate on another planet.
>
> The source of my information is a British official of Cabinet rank who prefers to remain unidentified. We believe on the basis of our inquiry thus far, that the saucers were staffed by small men – probably under four feet tall. It's frightening, but there is no denying the flying saucers come from another planet.
>
> This official quoted scientists as saying a flying ship of this type could not possibly been constructed on earth. The British Government, I learned, is withholding an official report on the flying saucer examination at this time, possibly because it does not wish to frighten the public…

The then editor of *Flying Saucer Review,* former pilot Derek Dempster, attempted to verify the account and contacted the London news editor of the International News Service, who replied: 'We tried hard to get the source of the story, but drew a blank.' Subsequent editor Gordon Creighton, a retired diplomat, also approached his own contacts to discover the identify the 'official of Cabinet rank' but to no avail. Kilgallen was not the sort of reporter to perpetuate a hoax. It is believed she too tried to follow up on what she had heard but there are no surviving papers to reveal the trails she followed or what she uncovered along the way.

Kilgallen carried on her investigative journalism for years afterwards, delving into numerous high-profile stories in search of the truth, none more so than the assassination of President John F. Kennedy on 22 November 1963. She published articles expressing scepticism of the conclusions of the Warren Report on the assassination and even secured the only interview with Jack Ruby during a recess at his trial for the murder of Lee Harvey Oswald. Her investigations clearly shook the American Secret Service, and both the FBI and CIA had files on Kilgallen. She was found dead in her Manhattan home on 8 November 1965. She had died from an overdose of alcohol and barbiturates. New York Medical Examiner James Luke suggested her death was 'accidental', but with no evidence of violence nor Kilgallen having been suicidal, the circumstances of her death remain undetermined. She was known to have compiled quite a dossier on the Kennedy assassination which, along with whatever she had uncovered about UFOs, could not be found among her files after her death.

Chapter 3

The 1950s

The object described in the national press as 'Britain's first flying saucer' was a 'strangely beautiful ... glistening silvery object' spotted at an estimated 3,000–4,000 feet over the King's Cross area of London shortly before 3 p.m. on 2 April 1950. It appeared to hover in the sky for a few minutes, then moved slowly in a north-easterly direction until it disappeared into clouds. The War Office and the Admiralty denied any knowledge of the object.

A spokesman for the Air Ministry's Meteorological Office in London confirmed they had been alerted to the object when numerous citizens started ringing them seeking an explanation, so their own experts 'had a good look at this mysterious object'. They were convinced it was not a meteorological balloon but could offer no explanation for what it was, adding candidly: 'Even among our own people there was disagreement as to what it could have been. One of the staff described it as pear-shaped. Another thought it had corners on it.' Indeed, a number of the witnesses on the street also commented on how the object seemed to change shape as they looked at it.

Later that same day, the Air Ministry was on the back foot and issued a statement claiming it was a balloon after all, adding that it had been used for parachute training and had broken loose from its moorings at RAF Weston-on-the-Green in Oxfordshire. Could the boffins at the Air Ministry's Meteorological Office really have got it so wrong?

Luminous Oval Over Preston

On Easter Sunday in 1950, 9 April, three Preston girls – Doris Wade, Lilian Spencer and Thirza Walkerdine – were walking along the Preston to Lancaster main road when they encountered a UFO. Doris Wade told a *Daily Mail* reporter: 'We saw what looked like a bright star in the east. It moved towards us in a north-westerly direction and as it steadily came nearer it took on an oval shape and looked quite big. It seemed to be luminous and was very bright. We watched it for quite a time until it disappeared into the clouds.' All three girls gave a similar description of what they saw. It certainly bears similarity to the object seen over London only a few days before.

The Ministry of Civil Aviation air traffic control station which was located at Barton Hall, only a few hundred yards away from where the girls saw the UFO, was approached for comment by a *Daily Herald* reporter. An official stated unequivocally, 'No balloons are released in this district' and pointed out 'if the object was moving to the north-west it was travelling in the teeth of a gale.' In other newspapers, including the *Daily Mail* and the *Daily Telegraph*, an unnamed Air Ministry meteorological forecaster was quoted offering an explanation for what the girls saw: 'It was a common error for people to speak of something travelling in a certain direction when they really meant that it was coming from that direction. If that was the case here it was possible that the object could have been a meteorological balloon blown over from Northern Ireland'. He also added the sun reflecting from its surface could make it look like 'a very bright star'.

The Heathrow Airport Sighting

On Sunday 5 November 1950 four members of staff at Heathrow (then known as London Airport) saw a UFO. Each one of them was qualified to make accurate observations of aerial phenomena. Fred Wilkinson, who had served five years as a flight engineer in the RAF, was a member of the Pan American Airways operational staff at the airport, and recalled: 'About 7.00pm I was on the ramp supervising preparations for a Transatlantic flight when I saw a lighted body coming from east to west at terrific speed. I thought at first it was a jet but then I saw that its shape, light and the presence of a blue flame from the tail made that impossible. It flew in a straight line. It did not describe a curve, as a shooting star, comet or rocket would. I would put the speed at about 1,000 mph.'

Former RAF gunner Patrick Maloney had also worked for Pan American for four years and also saw the UFO: 'It was going east to west and much too close to be a shooting star. It was a bright white light, metallic coloured, elongated but as it went out of sight it seemed to become spherical. There was no noise.' Another witness was former anti-aircraft gunner Fred Perrior who added: 'It was cigarette shaped when I first saw it. It was not a jet aircraft, nor was it a shooting star or comet. Before it disappeared it looked flat and round.'

Nearby was Mr E. Newman, a Pan American Airways maintenance man who had eight years in air service, who commented: 'I put it as a bluish-green light lasting for a few second. It travelled on a straight line. I am dead sure it was no aircraft or meteor.'

The Barrow-in-Furnace Silver 'Cigar' UFO

Just before noon on Tuesday 7 November 1950, Leslie Docker, the director of a firm of fruiterers, spotted 'a huge thing shaped like a cigar' emerging from the clouds in the west from the window of his office on Hindpool Road, Barrow-in-Furness, Cumbria. Estimating it to be about 100 feet long and 4,000 feet up, the end of the object 'looked darker than its centre which was an aluminium colour'. It appeared to be moving through broken cloud at about 80 mph. Ex-RAF man John Clarke of Geneva Street, Barrow, also saw the object. His description tallied with that of Mr Docker, adding that he was convinced it was too big to be any aeroplane.

The Benenden Blue Sphere

Second World War veteran Wing Commander Denis H. Carey (fifty-one) was driving his small van towards Sandhurst, not far from his home at Benenden, Kent, at 6.24 p.m. on Tuesday 14 November 1950 when a spherical object of a blue colour 'the shade you see on a television screen' streaked across the sky 1¼ miles ahead of him from west to east in the direction of the Strait of Dover. Wing Commander Carey was convinced it was not a comet, adding: 'It was certainly not an aircraft of any type that flies over Britain. It was travelling several times as fast as the fastest jet planes.'

Shoppers Spot UFO Over Hazel Grove

On 30 December 1950, newspapers carried the story of how women customers outside a butcher's shop in the village of Hazel Grove, Cheshire, stopped in their tracks when a flying saucer was spotted overhead at a height of around 2,000 feet, remaining visible for around two minutes. Alan Heyward (twenty-one), who worked in the shop, told a reporter: 'I saw a great circle hovering in the sky. It was silver on the rim and dark in the centre. Then it rose up at a terrific speed and disappeared.' A flying control officer at the A. V. Roe's Woodford airfield 2 miles away stated it was none of their aircraft, adding that at the time visibility was down to a mile because of haze.

'Silver Shillings' Over Suffolk

Suffolk botanist and ornithologist Irene Stubbings was looking out of the window of her lodgings on Cauldwell Avenue in Ipswich one Thursday lunchtime in January 1951 when her attention was caught by two silver objects in the sky: 'They looked for all the world like two silver shillings, one following the other, and they did not appear to be going exceptionally fast. I had them in full view for half a minute before they disappeared out of sight over the trees. They seemed to be flying very high and were travelling in a perfectly straight line. They were completely silent and were travelling in a south-westerly direction.'

Silvery-white 'Rugby Ball' Over Blackheath

Mrs Monica Manders was with her parents in the garden of her home on Shooters Hill Road, Blackheath, London, in September 1951 when they saw a curious object in the sky:

> It appeared to be a solid object, flying very high, travelling slowly. It was oblong, roughly the shape of a rugby ball and to us even at that height, it appeared to be two thirds the size of a rugby ball. It shone silvery white and was clear and distinct.
>
> It was in full sight for two or three minutes and immediately it disappeared from our view to the south another approached along the same route. In all we watched quite 20 of these mysterious objects, all following the same route. They came from the north-east, passed over Blackheath and when some distance away they swung sharply southwards and disappeared ... Their progress appeared slow to us, but that was undoubtedly due to the great height at which they were flying. They were completely silent. They looked like small oblong airships but with nothing suspended beneath them. [Author's note: Sounds like an early description of what we recognise today as 'tic-tac' UFOs]

The Exercise Mainbrace Incident

The headlines of the *Sunday Despatch* declared 'Saucer Chased RAF Jet Plane' and posed the question: what intruded into Exercise Mainbrance? Those who sighted the UFO on Friday 19 September 1952 consisted of two RAF officers and three aircrew as they stood near Coastal Command Shackleton Squadron HQ (No. 18 Group Coastal Command) at Topcliffe in Yorkshire. They had just landed after a flight and were watching a Meteor jet fighter coming in to land at the neighbouring Dishforth RAF station when they spotted a silvery-white object in pursuit of the Meteor. Those who saw the UFO were named in the press as Flight Lieutenant John W. Kilburn, Flight Lieutenant Marian Cybulski, Sergeant Flight Engineer Thomas Dewys, Master Signaller Albert Thompson and Leading Aircraftman George Grime. Flight Lieutenant John W. Kilburn (thirty-one), a native of Egremont, Cumberland, spoke for the group when he told a reporter what he saw:

> [It was] something different from anything I have ever seen in 3,700 hours of flying in a variety of conditions ... It was 10.53am on Friday. The Meteor was coming down from about 5,000 feet. The sky was clear. There was sunshine and unlimited visibility. The Meteor was crossing from East to West when I noticed the object in the sky. This object was silver and circular in shape, about 10,000 feet up, some five miles astern of the aircraft. It appeared to be travelling at a lower speed than the Meteor but was on the same course. I said 'What the hell's that?' and the chaps looked to where I was pointing. Somebody shouted it might be the engine cowling of the Meteor falling out of the sky. Then we thought it might be a parachute but as we watched, the disc maintained a slow forward speed for a few seconds before starting to descend. While descending it was swinging in a pendulum fashion from left to right, rather like a falling sycamore leaf.
>
> As the Meteor turned to start its landing run the object appeared to be following it but after a few seconds it stopped its descent and hung in the air as if rotating on its own axis.
>
> Then suddenly it accelerated at an incredible speed to the west, turned south-east then disappeared. As it went across to the west in a slow turn, the object seemed to change its shape to become more oval in appearance. It is difficult to estimate the object's speed. It was considerably faster than a shooting star. The incident happened within a matter of 15 to 20 seconds.
>
> During the few seconds that it was rotating we could see it was flashing in the sunshine. To us it appeared to be about the size of a Vampire jet aircraft. We are all convinced that it was a solid object. We realised very quickly that it could not be a broken cowling or a parachute. Nor do we believe that it was a small object like a meteorological balloon at a few hundred feet. I have no theories. I can only say what I saw.

A spokesman at the NATO Exercise Mainbrace Headquarters in Pitrivie, Fifeshire, refused to commit himself on whether the report was regarded as a serious one, but added: 'It is being investigated.' The Air Ministry refused to comment.

In the wake of the publicity and concern generated in official quarters by the Exercise Mainbrace incident, Prime Minister Winston Churchill wrote a personal note on 6 August 1952 to Secretary of State for Air Lord Cherwell, enquiring: 'What does all this stuff about flying saucers amount to? What can it mean? What is the truth? Let me have a report at your convenience.' The report and its content have still not been released to the British public.

RAF Pilots Spot Flying Saucers, 1952

On the afternoon of 21 October 1952, instructor Flight Lieutenant (later Air Commodore) Michael Swiney and trainee pilot Lieutenant David Crofts took off in a Gloster Meteor VII on a training flight from the RAF Central Flying School at Little Rissington in the Cotswolds. At 15,000 feet, just as they passed through a layer of cloud, Swiney spotted three white saucer-shaped objects which he pointed out to Crofts; the pair estimated them to be at 35,000 feet. Initially, the pilots thought the objects might have been three parachutes, but they appeared to remain stationary. As they continued to climb towards them the objects appeared more like flat tea saucers, were off-white in colour and appeared to have an iridescent light around their edges.

The three objects crossed over the path of the Meteor from left to right and would remain there. There was no indication of how they were powered and no portholes could be seen on them. Swiney reported their course and what they had seen to air traffic control at Little Rissington and the pair kept the UFOs under observation until the pilots looked away briefly and when they returned their eyes to where the objects had been, they had simply disappeared. All in all, the objects had been in view for approximately ten minutes. The 'blips' of the UFOs had been spotted on screen at several radar establishments and two Meteors were scrambled from Tangmere to investigate. It is believed they followed the UFOs but failed to make contact before they disappeared.

An entry in the Operations Record Book of CFS Little Rissington for 21 October 1952 records the incident, adding that ATCC Gloucester reported radar plots that confirmed the sighting, but the Air Ministry were quick to dismiss the possibility that what the pilots had seen were 'extra-terrestrial objects'.

Fast Bright Light Over Coast

At a time when there were fresh scares over the danger posed by Soviet Russia, a bright light was spotted by numerous witnesses as it sped across the sky over East Anglia and the south coast on Saturday 22 November 1952. It raised concerns in the media over whether it was an aeroplane, rocket or even a guided missile. Charles Henderson witnessed it from his sister's home in Bognor Regis and told a reporter: 'It flashed across the sky almost before I had realised it was there; it gave off a tremendous light.' PC William Keates stated: 'I thought at first it was the headlamps of a car behind me. Then I turned around and realised that it was travelling horizontally in the sky. It looked like a tadpole with a moving tail. It lit up the whole town of Bognor.'

Mr W. Liggens, a milkman of Newport on the Isle of Wight, was delivering milk at 6 a.m. when he had been startled by the whole street lightening. For a moment he thought it was a trick of the moonlight until he saw the 'tadpole-like object' with a glowing green head and red tail as it swept across the sky and quickly out of sight.

PC Tony Cox and a colleague were just going on duty at 6 a.m. and also saw the sky light up over Chichester: 'We thought that sparks from an electric train must be the cause until we turned round and saw the queer thing speed across the sky to the north-east.'

An Air Ministry spokesman said: 'I know of no service plane which carries lights of the kind described by these observers.'

Saucers Over Merthyr Tydfil

The *Daily Mail* of 16 November 1952 reported flying saucers had been seen by a railway signalman and a police sergeant near Merthyr Tydfil, Glamorgan. Signalman Stanley Morgan saw 'a brilliant orange streamlined object' as he was walking to work at 5 a.m. He described what he saw as having a disc-shaped front and a long tail. Having watched it for several seconds, it then disappeared in the direction of the coast. Police Sergeant D. Jones of Ynysybwl, 12 miles from Merthyr, reported seeing a similar-shaped object travelling across the sky at an estimated 500 mph. The colour of this object appeared to be an ice-white blue and strongly reflected the rays of the sun.

Encounter at Elmstead

One night in October 1953, Mr P. W. A. Underwood was cycling back to his home at Elmstead, Sussex, after visiting his sick father. The road along which he was cycling commands a fine view across open countryside at the north face of the South Downs. About ¾ of a mile from Elmstead he became aware of a very bright light in the sky that was moving towards him, accompanied by a loud rushing sound, a noise, Mr Underwood pointed out, that was distinctly different from the roar of a jet plane. He went on the describe:

> The light became very intense, lighting up all the surrounding countryside and I saw it came from a very large circular object which I should estimate was perhaps 2,000 to 3,000 feet up. The blueish silvery light appeared to come from all over it and not from any one spot. It was not directed towards the ground. There seemed to be portholes. It was something like the drawings of saucers which I have seen and read about in the newspapers...there appeared to be a long trail of light passing out behind it. It moved across the sky a little way off. It was almost stationary for perhaps two minutes and I began to feel scared. Then suddenly it shot upwards at great speed and disappeared.

Exercise Dividend

A decade after the Second World War Royal Observer Corps observers were still using the codeword 'Pheno' for UFOs, it is known that there were several instances of reports being written up and submitted. Sadly, few of those reports have surfaced to date, but one notable instance is recorded by Brian Watson in his book *Some Kind of Club: A History of No 6 Group ROC Norwich* (1984):

> It occurred during Exercise Dividend in July 1954: Observer Potter was plotting at about 11.30pm when there were reports from seven posts across the Group in quick succession. A bright object had come over the North-west coast of Norfolk at about 6,000 feet and was travelling at what was calculated to be the incredible speed of 2,500 and 3,000 mph; in fact it was too fast to plot. When the craft was approximately over Dereham it did a 90 degree turn and went in the direction of Wells. About halfway between the two towns it shot up vertically and disappeared. The Operations Room was not full as it was not a busy period during the exercise but all those who were present were ordered to keep quiet about the incident.

Foo Fighter Over London?

At 10.15 p.m. on 25 May 1955, Mr R. Russell was watching an American B47 bomber flying steadily at an estimated 30,000 feet over

Alexandra Park, London. Suddenly, he noticed a single light coming in from the south-west and about 100 feet above the B47. Mr Russell initially thought it was a jet making an interception, but he soon realised the object was no aircraft; instead, it was a clearly defined luminous disc or ball, which glowed amber red in colour and around the size of a pea when held at arm's length. It left no vapour trail, nor did it make any noise. When it was immediately above the aircraft the UFO suddenly stopped, stood still and about five seconds later it sped off at a speed Mr Russell estimated to be between 250 and 300 mph.

After covering a short distance south-east, it suddenly reversed direction and moved the same distance to the north-west. It suddenly stopped again and remained stationary for eight seconds, then shot off at a speed he believed would have been in excess of 900 mph. Meanwhile, apparently unperturbed by what had appeared near it, the B47 had not deviated from its course.

Trawler Crew Spot UFO Over the North Sea

The crew of the Lowestoft motor fishing trawler *Grasby* were on the North Sea some 130 miles off Smith's Knoll and 20 miles from the Dutch coast at 4 p.m. on 5 June 1955 when they spotted a UFO at least 10,000 feet above them. Skipper John Howard, a wartime recipient of the Distinguished Service Cross, reported the details to *The Eastern Evening News*, stating:

> When I first spotted the object I shouted to the Third Hand, Martin Spalding, and the deck hand on duty. They saw it too. It looked to me like a shining shilling. I got my binoculars on it as I spotted it on the starboard quarter. Its speed was so great that within five minutes it had flashed across the clear sky till it was on our starboard bow and had disappeared … I am satisfied that it was no plane. I can only think from what I have read about flying saucers that it must have been something of that character. It must have been going faster than any aircraft I have ever known or dreamed of.

Third Hand Spalding confirmed he had seen the same thing and was entered into the trawler's log as a true account of what they witnessed.

Near Collision of Meteor Jet Fighter with a UFO

Flight Lieutenant Jimmy Saladin reported for duty with 604 County of Middlesex Squadron, Royal Auxiliary Air Force on 14 October 1954 and took off in a Meteor Mk 8 jet fighter on a routine flight into a blue and cloudless sky. Climbing in a southerly direction towards the Thames Estuary, he saw two more Meteors in formation high above him. Keeping his eyes on the two fighters, checking his position and glancing at his instruments, Saladin noted his altimeter was showing he was just over 16,000 feet. Southend was almost beneath him when he spotted two circular objects which he described as 'one silvery and the other gold in colour' streaking between the two Meteors in the opposite direction. He observed the UFOs until they were high on his port beam and disappeared beyond his range of vision.

Saladin was to suffer a far greater shock when he returned to look through his windscreen and saw another object heading directly towards his aircraft. As it closed in, the object suddenly veered off and passed by on his port side. Saladin recalled: 'The thing had a bun-shaped top, a flange like two saucers in the middle and a bun underneath ... It was silvery in colour and could not have been far off because it overlapped my windscreen ... It was travelling at a tremendous speed. I was so shaken I had to fly around quietly for about ten minutes to recover.'

After radioing a report of the incident to control tower, he managed a safe landing but was left with the lasting regret that, having the object directly in his sights, he did not press the camera-gun button.

Southend UFO Terror

The *News Chronicle* of 16 October 1954 carried the following report:

> Patricia Hennessey (23) is scared. She is convinced that she has seen a flying saucer – on the ground. It terrified her and sent her running home trembling with fear. At first she would not talk about it, but gradually her family and friends persuaded her to tell what she saw.
>
> Miss Hennessey was walking in Park Lane, Southend, on her way home to nearby Chase Road just before midnight on Thursday 14 October when she was confronted by an object lying stationary in the centre of the roadway ... about 12ft tall. It was domed and cylindrical – about 10ft across. A pipe the thickness of a human body and rather like a gas mask tube came from inside the thing. It was attached down one side and went back in again at the bottom. It had no legs or wheels. There were no markings. It seems as though the Thing had a pale light shimmering from inside. I began to tremble. I turned and ran.

Miss Hennessey made detour of about a mile to get to her home. She arrived in a distressed condition and would comment to a *Southend Times* reporter: 'The object was so bright that the glare blinded me ... It terrified me and I got away from it as quickly as I could.'

The *News Chronicle* article continued: 'The spot is by the gates of Southchurch Hall Park. At the nearest house a woman was asked if she had seen any strange object the night before. She did not ask why she was being questioned. "I kept my curtains shut close last night" she answered, and would say no more.

Only 100 yards away from Cheltenham Road a woman reported seeing an airborne saucer a few months ago which was also seen and logged at Southend Airport as an unidentified object.'

The Ranton Encounter

Mrs Jessie Roestenburg was living a quiet life with her Dutch husband Tony, who had settled in Britain after the Second World War, and their three children – sons Anthony (eight), Ronald (six) and little daughter Karin (two) – in an isolated cottage at Vicarage Farm House in the rural village of Ranton, Staffordshire, until the afternoon of 21 October 1954. It was about 4.45 p.m. and her two sons were just back from school when they heard what sounded like an aircraft crashing; Mrs Roestenburg described it as sounding like 'a huge kettle pouring water upon a mighty fire'. One of the boys cried 'It's a jet' and they rushed outside where they spotted a very large object moving slowly overhead towards the south. Rushing around the side of the house to see where it went, they were startled to see nothing in the sky until they turned around and, to their shock and awe, they saw the craft was hovering over their home.

Rooted to the spot, Jessie tried to take in what she was seeing: 'I can only describe [the UFO] as a huge Mexican hat ... It must have been fifteen to twenty yards from where I stood. It covered the roof, so in circumference it must have been about sixty feet, it was enormous.' The object appeared to be made of a 'dull silver metal' that shone in the afternoon light with an outer rim that rotated as it hovered silently above the house. Above the lower body of the craft was a dome; the back was the colour of aluminium and the front consisted of two transparent panels with two figures behind them. The UFO was slightly tilted towards the ground, clearly so they could get a better view. Mrs Roestenburg and the occupants regarded each other.

Jessie recalled they looked very much like human men – she could see them from their waist to their head. They were 'very beautiful' with white skin and long shoulder-length blonde hair but their foreheads seemed unusually high. They were dressed in turquoise blue outfits that resembled ski suits. Jessie was particularly struck by the unsmiling expressions of sadness or compassion on their faces. Terrified, Mrs Roestenburg's two boys threw themselves onto the ground and the family dog that had accompanied them outside ran off yelping down the farm track to the village.

As Jessie stared, transfixed, it began to move, flashing a purple light from the front as it did so and it started to ascend at an angle of 45 degrees. Jessie found she could move again, so she checked on her children and then ran into the house to grab a pencil and paper and sketch what she and her children had seen. Returning outside, she saw the UFO coming back from north to south. It circled the house anti-clockwise three times then shot up skywards and away.

Before her death in 2017 Mrs Roestenburg retold her story many times for newspapers, magazine articles, books and television programmes including *Arthur C Clarke's Mysterious World*. All who met her believed Jessie Roestenburg to be an ordinary housewife and mother who never had a particular fascination in UFOs but was a truthful witness to one of the most extraordinary British UFO encounters of the twentieth century.

Encounter at Kirkcudbrightshire

Forestry Commission mechanic Maurice Brazier (thirty-two) was driving home from Newton Stewart along a deserted road to New Galloway, Kirkcudbrightshire, Scotland, during the closing months of 1955. It was 7.30 p.m. when he saw a bright light on the hillside which he assumed was headlamps from an oncoming car which he fully expected to meet at the approaching corner. Instead of a car he encountered a large, illuminated object hovering approximately 40 feet above the road. Maurice initially thought it might be a helicopter with a mountain rescue unit but as it closed in, it soon became apparent the object was of a large elliptical shape, some 60 feet in length, and had bluish lights along the side.

Badly shaken by what had confronted him, Brazier stopped his van and leaped out. The UFO kept moving until it was about 20 yards from him and it banked away to his left. Only then was he able to see the UFO was in fact a huge double saucer with lights along the outer rim that appeared to revolve clockwise, with an inner 'drum' of a metallic colour that reflected the lights.

He arrived home twenty minutes later, pale and agitated, he would admit 'If ever I had a fright, it was that night.' Although no one else came forward to say they had witnessed the same thing that night, a forestry worker from Dalmacullum witnessed a 'weird-looking object' rising from the hills one morning. Others also came forward with their accounts of UFOs over the area, including New Galloway garage proprietor Mr H. McWilliam who had spotted a 'red orb that flashed across the sky' while travelling through the hills a few months earlier.

UFO Over the National Gliding Championships

As Britain's gliding champion Philip Wills was in the air during the National Gliding Championships over Lasham airfield, Hampshire, in June 1955. Yvonne Bonham, secretary of the British Gliding Association, and other officials watching his flight noticed a 'boomerang-shaped object' hovering above him. Estimated to have been around 3,000 feet up and appearing to be dark against the sky, the object was estimated to have been about 40 feet from tip to tip. It hovered for about thirty seconds and then sped off at high speed in a north-westerly direction. The sighting was reported to the Air Ministry who ruled out the likelihood of the UFO being a shadow, but a meteorologist was quoted in the press offering a possible explanation: 'If people watch a glider for some time the image can stay in the mind for some minutes afterwards.'

Mystery Lights Over Birmingham

Several UFOs, seen to be 'glowing with incandescent light', were spotted flying over Birmingham at 7.30 p.m. on 26 August 1955. Former Royal Naval Volunteer Reserve Lieutenant-Commander Denis Thursfield spotted about fifteen mysterious craft travelling across the sky in formation from the north-west on a southerly course at a remarkably high speed at about 20,000 feet. Thursfield was convinced they were not any known aircraft because they glowed with an incandescent light that was still visible when they went behind clouds, left only minimal vapour trails behind them and made no sound at all.

The Glenlean Bus Sighting

Ten student passengers, driver John Black and science master John Ferguson on the Colintraive–Dunoon bus in Argyll, Scotland, which carries students and teachers to the local grammar school, spotted a UFO on 7 September 1955. Mr Ferguson recalled it had been while the bus was travelling through Glenlean, around 7 miles from Dunoon. He had seen five UFOs in the sky to the west. Each consisting of two flat half circles, bright as though they were made from aluminium, they reflected the rays of the sun. Unfortunately, the bus was travelling in the opposite direction, so it was not possible to ascertain if they were hovering or moving.

UFO Over Wolverhampton

At 10.45 p.m. on 14 June 1956 many people spotted a yellow disc that shone like a star over Wolverhampton. Coming from the north, it hung over the town until it 'faded like a light bulb going out slowly'. Several minutes later it reappeared towards the south of the town and slowly moved towards the southern horizon where it was lost to sight at 11.30 p.m. In an attempt to explain what had been seen, USAF Headquarters stated the following day that refuelling exercises had been taking place over the West Midlands at the time of the sighting. The meteorological station at Elmden Airport, Birmingham, suggested it may have been a weather balloon. An official stated that a balloon of some 6 feet across was released at Liverpool at 9 p.m. every night and it could have been carried over Wolverhampton by prevailing winds. The Fazakerley meteorological station who release the balloons, however, quashed the theory when they revealed their balloon had burst at 9.41 p.m. that night when just 10 miles from Liverpool. And could slow-travelling jets out on a refuelling exercise really look like a bright star?

UFOs Over Cheltenham

Mr H. Vallincourt of Bishop's Cleeve spotted a huge UFO over Cleeve Hill, Cheltenham, in June 1956. He described its size as 'Ten times the size of any existing aircraft ... looking like the Queen Mary at a distance of two or three miles.' One of the most famous ships of the day, the RMS *Queen Mary* was 1,019.4 feet (310.7 metres) long. 'The object was blazing with light which came from inside and showed through extremely large square windows. After hovering for about 10 minutes it moved off in the direction of Charlton Kings. It stopped then restarted, this time going in the direction of Gloucester. For the whole of the time there was not a sound.' At 11.15 p.m. Mr H. Hands was looking out of the bedroom window of his home on Mead Road, Leckhampton, when he spotted an object that 'looked like a star but was eight or nine times bigger' in the sky midway between Stroud and Gloucester. The object had been stationary when he first spotted it, but it then moved towards the horizon and gradually got lower and lower until it could be seen no more.

Sidney Hale of Apperley was another eyewitness who spotted an object in the sky, which he described as 'out of this world', when he was leaving the British Messier Ltd factory on the Cheltenham–Gloucester Road at 11.30 p.m. Curiously, a few nights before these sightings, Mr Ken Karling of Hester's Way, Cheltenham, had seen what he could only describe as 'a terrific beam of light in the sky, which made no noise and disappeared off in the direction of Gloucester'.

The Bentwaters-Lakenheath Incident

The evening of 13 August 1956 had been dry and pretty much clear in the beautiful, wide-open sky over Suffolk. Those who took time to look up noted the large number of shootings stars that night, but then it was the right time of year for Perseid meteor showers to be seen.

At 9.30 p.m. radar operators at RAF Bentwaters (RAF base but tenanted by the USAF) saw an object appear on their screens that was approaching rapidly from over the sea. Initially it appeared to be a perfectly normal aircraft return, but it appeared to be travelling at several thousand miles per hour.

A group of objects were also detected moving at a slow speed in the north-east of the screens. This grouping appeared to merge into a single, very large object before it left the screens in a northerly direction. At the same time another fast-moving object was seen traversing the sky from east to west.

A T-33 training aircraft from 512th Fighter Interceptor Squadron crewed by Lieutenants Charles Metz and Andrew Rowe was instructed to investigate but did not make a visual sighting. At 10.55 p.m. an object was detected approaching Bentwaters from an easterly direction, travelling at an estimated speed of 2,000–4,000 miles per hour. It faded from the radar screen as it passed over the base, then reappeared to the west. As the object was logged on the radar screens a white light moving at a tremendous speed was spotted by observers on the ground and the pilot of a C-47 flying at 4,000 feet over Bentwaters reported a similar light as it passed under his aircraft.

Bentwaters then alerted the USAF at Lakenheath to what had been happening and to keep a sharp look-out. Ground crew at Lakenheath would subsequently report visual sightings of several luminous objects in the sky that night. In a particularly curious sighting, two glowing objects, estimated to be about the size of a golf ball held at arm's length, were spotted arriving, changing course then appeared to merge together before moving off again.

Technical Sergeant Forrest Perkins was the Watch Supervisor in the Lakenheath Radar Air Traffic Control centre on the night of the incident. In a 1968 letter to the Condon Committee (the University of Colorado UFO Project run under the direction of physicist Edward Condon, funded by the United States Air Force from 1966 to 1968) Perkins claimed that two RAF De Havilland Venom interceptors had been scrambled to intercept the object that had appeared on radar near Lakenheath. According to Perkins, one of the Venoms had to turn back due to engine problems but the other achieved contact. The object, however, outmanoeuvred him and appeared behind the aircraft.

Although not appearing to be aggressive, the object remained about ¼ of a mile behind the Venom despite the pilot taking evasive action to shake it off his tail. Perkins described the pilot as 'getting worried, excited and also pretty scared'. After ten minutes the object suddenly quit its pursuit and hovered stationary in the sky. The pilot of the Venom saw his chance to make some distance between himself and the object, but as his aircraft was running low on fuel he returned to base. The object soon sped north at an incredible speed, but 'echoes' of it remained on radar screens until 3.30 a.m.

The sequence of events on the night over the Bentwaters and Lakenheath air bases on 13 August 1956 were recorded in the original USAF Project Blue Book. In its analysis of the incident the Condon report concluded: 'Although conventional or natural explanations cannot be ruled out, the probability of such seems low in this case and the probability that at least one genuine UFO was involved appears to be fairly high.'

'Blip' on the South Coast

At 10 p.m. on 30 August 1956 RAF Fighter Command radar stations in London spotted a 'blip' on their screens which could not be accounted for. Half an hour later, a Meteor crew preparing to land at West Malling, Kent, saw 'an odd light' in the sky.

Flight Lieutenant Harry Goldstone, the navigator of a MkXI Meteor, related: 'We were at about 2,000ft. The light was a few thousand feet above us, but it didn't have a star's intensity of light. I don't subscribe to flying saucers, but I don't know what this light was. Nor does anyone else.'

Ground control replied that they too could see it, but they could not identify it. Jet aircraft were sent to investigate; their tracks were plotted right through the blip, but crew reported that they had not seen anything. Search planes were sent up to fly at 6,000 feet and above in case the object was a balloon trailing cables. The Air Ministry had no report of a balloon breaking away.

UFO Over Lincolnshire

A UFO was seen high in the sky by thousands who were strolling along on the promenade at the popular seaside resort of Cleethorpes, Lincolnshire, on the afternoon of 22 September 1956. The sky was clear and blue and the mysterious spherical object, described as 'looking like a glass globe with something white inside it', hovered at an estimated 54,000 feet for about an hour, despite the wind being more than 40 mph at that altitude at the time. The object was also picked up on radar and two fighter aircraft were scrambled to investigate, but by the time they arrived the object had gone. A Meteorological Office spokesman from nearby at RAF Manby had studied the object through a telescope and estimated it to have a diameter of 80 feet and stated 'It certainly is not a balloon from here.'

One UFO Becomes Three Over Redcar

On 16 May 1957 people out on the promenade at Redcar spotted three bright white illuminated objects below a low cloud belt over Tees Bay. People were able to observe the UFOs for about four minutes before they sped off towards the east at a fantastic speed. Redcar newsagent Mr W. Smith was among the watchers and told a reporter that it seemed as if a single bright light had split – first into two and then into three parts. 'The three lights came towards us and then sped off towards Marske.'

At Ormesby, Malcolm Fixter and a number of his friends spotted what he described as three glowing discs from Woodley Grove. At Hartlepool, police did make some enquiries after receiving reports of the lights in the sky in case they were flares from a vessel in distress. While in West Hartlepool Mr A. T. Gyllenspetz was leaving his daughter's house on Thornville Road and saw the three lights hovering in the sky for a few seconds before they sped off out to sea. In an interview he added that they looked solid but were not aircraft.

UFO Over Bletchley

Bletchley Park is famous for being the Government Code and Cypher School where Alan Turing and his team broke the German Enigma code. It was established as the National Technical Authority for information security during the Second World War. After the end of the conflict, as Britain entered into the Cold War, what was by that time known as GCHQ moved to Eastcoat but the site remained active and was occupied by several government organisations. Consequently, it can be easily imagined that some consternation was caused when a UFO was first spotted at about 3.30 p.m. on 22 May 1957 as it hovered over Bletchley Park and the nearby town of Bletchley.

One woman who witnessed the UFO told a reporter: 'It was like a short, fat, cigar hanging vertically.' The account, published in *Flying Saucer Review*, added: 'School children studied the silver object and shops emptied of customers who hurried out onto the streets to stare at the mystery craft.'

Despite a strong breeze, the UFO remained stationary for over an hour until around 5.10 p.m. when the craft suddenly changed to a horizontal position and flashed out of sight at an incredible speed in the direction of Leighton Buzzard.

'Tadpoles' Over Mansfield

Three colleagues from an office and a young girl spotted tadpole-like dark shapes in the sky in a westerly direction towards Sutton-in-Ashfield on 11 February 1957. One in the group was Royal Photographic Society associate Mr G. H. Allison, who first spotted the five objects – two large, three small – from a bus he was travelling on going home after work. He described them as being stationary, silhouetted against the clear sky for three minutes. The two larger objects then broke formation, moving off almost vertically and leaving contrails behind them. The five objects then shot across the sky at great speed in a north-westerly direction, disappearing from sight over the Pleasley area.

Mr A. Gell and his family who lived in nearby Aspley also witnessed the tadpole-like objects on 11 February, but only saw four – two large and two small – and spotted them again on the following night of 12 February: 'They were definitely not aircraft. They remained stationary for two to two and a half minutes, and then dashed off at a terrific speed. They were large and black and left a vapour trail behind them.'

Radar Picks Up UFO Over Scotland

At noon on Thursday 4 April 1957, two separate radar sets (and their duplicates) operated by civilians at the Ministry of Supply at Luce Bay registered a UFO over the west coast of Scotland which remained on screen for some time. Estimated to have been some 60,000 feet in the air, it was 'too fast, too big and too manoeuvrable to be a plane'. Air Ministry Intelligence were informed, and a full detailed report was sent to London to be studied by top-level radar and intelligence officers. Wing Commander Walter Whitworth, commanding officer at the RAF bomber trails range at West Freugh, stated: 'I have been ordered by the Air Ministry to say nothing about the object. I am not allowed to reveal its position, course and speed. From the moment of picking it up it was well within our area. It was an object of some substance – quite definitely not a freak. No mistake could have been made by the civilians operating the sets. They are fully qualified and experienced officers.'

James Emmerson (forty-four), a lorry driver from Collin, Dumfriesshire, claimed he saw the object a few hours before it was picked up on the radar screens when he was on the road about 30 miles south of Penrith at 11.30 on the night of Wednesday 3 April: 'I noticed a reflection on the windscreen. I thought at first it was another vehicle's headlights but nothing appeared on the road. I stopped my lorry, drew into the side and switched off my headlights.' It was then he noticed a UFO hovering above him. 'It was a perfect half moon, but it has a distant gold rim with a straight edge on top.'

On 5 April, the day after the radar sighting, John Anderson, an iron moulder of Culloden Street, Glasgow, saw two objects 'like two silver threepenny bits' hovering over the city suddenly disappear shortly after he noticed them. He thought it might have been a trick of the light but there was not a cloud in the sky.

A further sighting in the area came on Sunday 7 April when two golfers at Rothesay, Isle of Bute, reported they had seen three circular objects in the sky. One of the witnesses, Mr J. McLellan described what he saw: 'They were round and gave off a brilliant, silvery glow. They were in a line and flying high and fast.'

Flying Saucers Over Sheffield

At 8.20 p.m. on Monday 17 June 1957, Barnsley resident Mrs Watkyn spotted a small light in the sky which shot downwards like a meteor until it was just above the rooftops, where it disappeared behind the houses. Then a long, thin, golden cone with a disc at its head pointing downwards was seen to float downwards to the left of the first light, then it too disappeared behind houses. Around the same time, roughly 16 miles away, Miss Anne Norwood, her mother, her aunt and several of their neighbours on their street witnessed an almost identical phenomena over Firth Park, Sheffield.

Two days later, Mrs Toni Salveta and her son were walking along Paradise Street in Sheffield at around 8 p.m. when they spotted 'two silver white discs, rather like doughnuts' in the sky. They estimated these to be about 20 feet in diameter and moving gently along at about 40 mph. The two objects were seen edgeways and tipped over, so they appeared circular. The couple watched them until the objects disappeared behind the Don Picture Palace. When they emerged again, the discs had appeared to have slid together and were now forming a single circle. On that same evening, Hester Rodgers and her friend Barbara Visick were some 7 miles away bird watching in woods near Totley Hall Domestic Science Training College. The pair noticed a brilliant silvery disc in the sky. Both were struck by the brilliance of the object and the silence which accompanied it.

Acting on a hunch that something may manifest again, Mrs Salvetas and her son returned to Paradise Street at 8 p.m. on Friday 21 June. After ten minutes or so a large yellow-orange disc with what appeared to be a fin appeared in the sky. 'Then out of an orange cloud emerged a saucer, complete with three landing domes, with two smaller discs apparently sliding in and out of it, whilst yet another disc to the top left of the large slip seemed to stand guard.' The following evening the Salvetases returned with their friend and local ufologist Philip Rodgers, who compiled a special report on this week of sightings for *Flying Saucer News*. On his last night the group saw several outlines of two small greyish discs, but at 8.20 p.m. came a brief glimpse of a brilliant silvery disc as it rapidly floated across the sky.

UFO Over RAF A-Bomber Base

On Monday 21 October 1958, a UFO was spotted and tracked on radar flying slowly over RAF Gaydon in Warwickshire. Particular concern was raised at this apparent aerial intruder because this base was one of the RAF's atomic bomber stations where aircrew were trained to serve on Valiants. Flying Officer D. W. Sweeney was in the air flying a Meteor on a training exercise from RAF North Luffenham in Rutland. He was flying at 28,000 feet over Gaydon when he nearly collided with an object in the airspace. As he approached the UFO from the starboard side, its lights were suddenly extinguished and it disappeared.

Landing at Tarland

The windswept and challenging Aberdeen countryside between Braemar and Ballatar, east of the Cairngorm mountains, has been a popular area for military training for many years. During a Territorial Army weekend exercise a few miles outside the village of Tarland in November 1958, two young soldiers were given the duty of occupying a small hilltop. They had full equipment with them and dug a trench to shelter in. At first light the soldiers heard a strange 'gurgling' sound from behind some trees a few hundred yards from their position. The noise persisted and the soldiers decided to go and investigate. As they approached, the source of the gurgling emerged in the form of two 7- or 8-foot-tall beings talking to each other. They were described as being 'dressed peculiarly' and appeared to find it difficult to walk over the rough hilltop.

Initially transfixed by fear at what they were seeing, the two young soldiers suddenly snapped out of it and ran down the hillside to seek help in Tarland. When they reached the road to the village, they heard a 'swishing' noise behind them. Upon turning around, they saw 'a huge, brilliant object' coming up behind them, just a few feet off the road. The soldiers ran hard and the UFO swooped up and over their heads, pulsating as it did so and leaving a shower of sparks behind it. It then disappeared skyward, leaving two very shaken young soldiers in its wake.

UFO Landing and Occupants Seen at Stratford-upon-Avon

Leonard Hewins, who worked as a general labourer for Stratford-upon-Avon Corporation, had finished work for the day in January 1959 and was collecting his bicycle from the rear of the refuse tip near the car park on Arden Street when his attention was caught by a glowing, round, red object travelling slowly towards him from the east. The object came to rest near a tennis court around 100 yards away from Mr Hewins. The glowing light went out and a 12-foot-high blue haze formed just above the ground where the object was.

He then spotted three tall humanoid figures, which Mr Hewins estimated must have been around 10 feet tall, moving in the blue haze. He described how one of occupants had faced him and he could see them raise up their heads and arms, then, with a somewhat clumsy movement, the tall aliens appeared to step up, lifting themselves as if seating themselves on something.

Mr Hewins was transfixed by what he saw and found himself staring at the landed UFO and its occupants. He was unable to move until the blue haze rose slightly. The object began to glow with the same brilliance as before it landed, then sped off to the west. As it departed, he recalled 'beautiful stars shot out from the rear' and the craft emitted a sound like that you get 'when pressing your fingers in and out of your ears at a waterfall'.

The case was investigated by BUFORA area investigator John D. Llewellyn, who wrote up the story for *Flying Saucer News*. Mr Llewellyn was impressed by the candour of Mr Hewins, who he considered a reliable witness who had no desire to seek publicity but had been subjected to ridicule when relating his story to others.

Chapter 4
The 1960s

Flying Saucer Over Bolton

As many people made their way to work on the morning of Tuesday 17 January 1960, a UFO was spotted by tens of people over Bolton. Jimmy Gee was making deliveries in his butcher's van when he saw it, describing what he saw to a reporter: 'At first it looked like a slice of the moon. The long bright yellow strip, not unlike a fluorescent light, turned, dropped down horizontally and began to move in the direction of Walkden.' Mr Gee then carried on his journey towards Farnworth, but just two minutes later he spotted the UFO again, travelling at tremendous speed towards Manchester. Pulling in at a petrol station, both Mr Gee and the attendant watched the UFO, noting 'vapour jets' coming from underneath the saucer. Then, with a streak of flame, it zoomed up high into the atmosphere where it passed out of sight. About ten minutes later Mr Gee and others who had followed the progress of the UFO spotted a fast-moving jet plane travelling from where the object had disappeared across a quarter of the horizon to where he had first seen it. Witnesses were of the opinion that the RAF had also detected the object and had come to investigate.

The Minsterley Mystery

A police officer on a routine patrol sighted and reported a UFO over the village of Minsterley, near Shrewsbury, Shropshire, on 2 June 1960. Seen clearly, he estimated the object to be about 6,000 feet up in the sky over the village. An aircraft from RAF Shawbury was despatched to investigate, but it was reported that no craft was found in the airspace. An RAF spokesman offered the explanation that 'It could have been a weather balloon that had gone adrift.'

Landing at Westcliff-on-Sea

Mr C. Giddings of Ronald Park Avenue, Westcliff-on-Sea, Essex, was out walking his dog at 11.20 p.m. on Tuesday 7 June 1960 when he saw a green-glowing object, which he initially thought might have been a satellite, but the speed in which it was travelling in the five seconds it was visible as it flew from south-east to north-west made him reconsider what he was actually seeing. State-registered Nurse Beverly Acock of Kenilworth Gardens also saw the UFO descending towards earth giving off a bright blue light, making a whistling nose as it did so and leaving a trail of yellow light behind it. The object she saw was so bright it lit up the road and rooftops in the area and she was convinced it had actually landed.

'Giant Catherine Wheel' Over Boreham Wood

On 28 August 1960, Mrs Evelyn Aaron of Theobald Street, Boreham Wood, Hertfordshire, heard a strange, high-pitched sound. When she looked up to where the noise was coming from, she saw a circular object flying fast and low. A man walking by on the street also saw the object and shouted, 'Did you see that?' When this story was published in a local paper, Mrs E. Smith of Garefield House, Kilburn Park wrote in: 'The giant Catherine wheel seen over Boreham Wood was certainly no optical illusion. My neighbour and I saw a similar object pass over about three weeks ago at 2.15pm.'

The Tyneside Triangle

One of the shapes of UFOs that has come to prominence after a spate of sightings in both Britain and the USA in the 1980s are triangular UFOs; however, there are several earlier sightings, including 'a triangular formation of lights with a red light in the centre' which was seen by people in Consett, South Shields, Fawdon, and Fenham, Newcastle, on 8 September 1960.

Among the witnesses were Mr J. Leslie Otley, Secretary of the Tyneside UFO Society, his wife and two of their neighbours who saw the UFO between 9.15 and 9.40 circling over Deanham Gardens, Fenham. Mrs Otley stated she first saw a single red light in the sky, followed by a triangular formation of lights with a red light in the centre. After some twenty minutes the formation moved off in a northerly direction. On that same night Mr J. Bolt of Acorn Terrace, Red House Farm Estate, Fawdon, Newcastle, also spotted what he described as 'a ball of separate lights flashing, it circled over the estate and then disappeared to the north'. A spokesman at RAF Acklington stated he had received reports on the phenomena from at least two sources and these had been passed on to the Air Ministry, but added: 'I have no further information about this and even if I had we are not allowed to release information.'

White Object Over Warminster

The *Daily Express* of 12 November 1960 carried the story of an army officer and four camp guards at Warminster, Wiltshire, who all spotted a dazzling white object in the sky the previous night. It hovered for a few minutes then vanished into the night, leaving white sparks behind it.

Return of the Scareships?

Gordon Dewey was standing by Fry's factory at Keynsham in Bristol in November 1960 when a UFO sped over the sky above him with a 'whoosh'. He described the objects as being 'shaped like a long silver cigar' which left a white trail behind it, ending in red sparks. A spokesman from the nearby Filton Meteorological Office witnessed the UFO too, adding it flashed with a light so bright 'it illuminated the whole building, like a sudden shaft of moonlight'.

Another cigar-shaped object was seen over Gloucester by Mrs Iles of Uplands in the town at 8 a.m. on 12 November, who described it as 'a huge mass of light ... a huge cigar-shaped shape ... just like an airship'. She observed it fly from the south to the north-east from about a mile away.

Shining Object Over Shoreham

A 'shining object ... as bright as a very bright star and very high' was spotted by Auxiliary Coast Guard Albert Morris from his lookout at the entrance to Shoreham Harbour as it flashed over the Sussex coastline at dawn on 5 January 1961. Managing to focus his binoculars on the object, he followed it as it flew south to east where it disappeared after only four minutes, having covered a quarter of a compass, placing the speed the object was travelling in the region of 1,000 mph.

The Isle of Wight Sighting

Mrs Smith was visiting her daughter on the night of 3 July 1961. The pair were on the roof of the flat bringing in baby linen from the clothesline when Mrs Smith glanced out to sea where she spotted lights which she assumed were from a ship in the distance. Her daughter, however, pointed out that the lights could not be coming from a ship because they were actually in the air. As they watched, it seemed like the lights were coming closer and could be counted as five distinct lights in a row with another above the five. The lights got ever closer and soon the object they were part of could be discerned as it moved silently across the sky.

Mrs Taylor was so afraid at the approach of the UFO that she backed down the stairs, but was able to describe it as circular or saucer shaped with five porthole lights that emitted rays of orange-coloured light. There was also an orange-coloured diffused light on the top and the whole base appeared to glow with orange light. When it was around a quarter of a mile away the approaching UFO suddenly changed course and sped off in the direction from the which it had come; a glowing ring of light lingered where the UFO had been.

UFO Lights Over Hertfordshire

Peter Wilkinson and his girlfriend Josephine Steele had been watching the sunset on a park bench near Josephine's home in Stansted St Margarets, Hertfordshire, on a clear night on 30 June 1961 when they spotted two yellowish lights in the sky. They were rather like car headlights because they appeared to be linked somehow, but were far brighter than any car lights of the day. The couple both sprang to their feet, but the lights moved into the distance at a remarkable speed, veered to the right then disappeared. The couple were unnerved by what they had seen so they made for home, but after just a few yards the lights appeared again, this time much closer, and began to move towards the couple.

Peter and Josephine became more and more disturbed by what they were seeing, and they ran for a group of nearby houses. By that time the lights were down low and behind some trees but could still be seen, though they were no longer moving. When they got close to Josephine's home on Hoddeston Road they saw a group of six people talking at the roadside. The pair asked if they had seen the lights and they all agreed that they had seen the same pair of lights descend from the sky.

The sighting was confirmed by a group of six people consisting of Mrs J. Plumtree with her husband, father Mr R. H. Stevens, Mr and Mrs A. Fowler of Sheffield and Miss Mehinnick of Widbury Farm, who were at Butler's Hall, near Ware. They had all seen two bright yellow lights on the same evening.

The bright yellow lights appeared over the Widford area and were visible to the group for ten minutes until it appeared as if they had been switched off or departed at tremendous speed. The group also agreed the lights were intense and 'almost hurt our eyes to look at them'. Curiously, some twenty minutes later the lights were seen one last time in the same position by Mr Plumtree and Mr Fowler.

The Air Ministry was informed of the incident, commenting: 'I am afraid our men can throw no light on it. We doubt it was one of those radio-sonde balloons which are being sent up to collect data.'

Off the Coast of Essex

The *Daily Mail* of 7 July 1961 carried the story of a reliable report from a pilot cutter who had spotted an object as large as an aircraft crashing into the North Sea 20 miles from Walton-on-the-Naze, Essex, which led to a big air-sea rescue effort being launched, with cargo ships, a Royal Navy minesweeper and a helicopter sent to the scene to investigate. However, after checks were made with the RAF, USAAF and Civil Aviation authorities the return came back that no planes were known to be missing, so the search was called off.

Hovering UFO Slows Car

At 3.30 a.m. on the morning of Friday 9 February, Ronald Wildman was not long into his journey driving a Vauxhall Victor for delivery to Wales when, rounding a bend on the Irvinghoe–Tring road, he nearly ploughed into a large object that was hovering over the road. He did not need to hammer on the brakes, however, because as his car got closer to the object its engine progressively lost power, until it started stalling when he was about 20 feet from the craft.

Mr Wildman now had a chance to take in the details of the craft, which he estimated was 30–40 feet across with a curved or domed upper surface and a straight lower margin. There were about eight to ten dark, squarish portholes or vents at equal intervals along the lower part, close to the lower rim.

The UFO then moved away at about 20 mph and, after 50 yards, the object passed just above trees on the left-hand side of the road. Mr Wildman recalled the frost on the trees was then forced down onto the car 'like rain or hail' and a ring of vapour appeared on the lower margin of the object.

The UFO then accelerated away, upwards and to the right, and sped off at a fantastic speed. His car then picked up speed and ran normally again. Mr Wildman was considerably shaken by this experience, and he reported what had happened to the police.

Metamorphic UFO Over Lancashire

At 10.38 p.m. on the dark and wet night of 4 August 1962, Mr R. A. Bury (twenty-one) of Nelson, Lancashire, was on the road between Bacup and Burnley. Looking west, he spotted a rhomboid-shaped object in the sky above the horizon about 5 miles away and 3,000 feet high. Observed over the course of around four minutes, the UFO was seen to split into two triangular halves that then slowly morphed into ovoids. The objects then reunited and resumed its original shape. It then became a shapeless circular object that slowly moved up and down.

The movement was once up, then down slowly to its original position. It then split into two equal portions for about ten seconds before joining together again. The size was about that of a sixpence held at arm's length. While in view, the object apparently shrank to the size of a dot in a fraction of a second then suddenly resumed its original size.

Flying Saucers Over Durham

The *Sunderland Echo* of 2 September 1962 reported the story of three nurses who spotted a flying saucer when they looked out of a window at Ryhope General Hospital. They commented to a reporter: 'We thought it was a parachute at first but there was no man hanging from the straps.' Judith Loftus (twenty) of Station Estate North, Murton, added: 'The object remained poised over the grounds of the hospital for some seconds, shimmering in the sunshine. Then it raced behind a cloud.' In that same week Sunderland housewife Mrs Rita Hodgson saw a 'saucer' hovering over the sea while doing her washing. Another unnamed woman watched from her bedroom window for half an hour as 'a weird illuminated object danced in the sky'.

Glowing Box Over a Derbyshire Moor

Trainee teacher Michael Valentine (twenty) of Brampton left Glossop on the Chapel-en-le-Frith road shortly after 10 p.m. on Sunday 19 August 1962 and was crossing a Derbyshire moor when he noticed a strange glowing object in the sky. He described what he saw as 'box-shaped with rounded corners, it had three or four lighted windows and the whole was surrounded by a glowing light'. Michael estimated the height of the object as between 200 and 300 feet. Stopping the engine and opening the car window for a better look, he also noticed the object made no sound and showed no navigation lights. In the car with him was Maureen Rhodes of Spital, who also saw the UFO. They watched the object for two or three minutes until it disappeared from view.

UFO Scares Leicestershire Woman

Can you imagine being the passenger in a car and seeing something utterly beyond belief but the driver, rightly concentrating on driving, sees little or nothing of what you just saw? That is exactly what happened to Mrs Myra Jones of Norris Hill when she was the passenger of a car driven by her husband, Mr W. E. Jones, the clerk of Ashby Woulds UDC, on the evening of Thursday 13 September 1962. At 11.20 p.m. they were heading down a country lane on their journey from Overfield to Moira, on the border between Leicestershire and Derbyshire, when Myra became aware of a light over the car. She described what she had seen to the local press: 'Right above the car at about the height of the telegraph poles was a grey luminous object bigger than the car. It was curved underneath and the top was domed like a child's humming top. There were some dark spots round the rim of the base and the whole thing seemed to be tilted slightly and to be revolving slowly. I was absolutely terrified as I thought it was going to land on the bonnet of the car. After a few moments it made a swishing noise, like a rocket and disappeared.'

Meanwhile, Mr Jones was looking ahead at the road and did not see anything unusual. He told a *Northern Echo* reporter: 'I thought my wife had been taken ill – she was crouching in her seat and saying "Oh no, it can't be." When I slowed down she implored me to drive on quickly. She told me nothing of what she had seen until we reached our home a mile away. She was extremely upset and distressed.'

Orb Over Sheffield

From the *Sheffield Star* newspaper of 22 September 1962: 'A mysterious glowing white 'pearl in the sky' has been seen by as least twelve people over Worksop and Manton colliery. The sightings have been described by eyewitnesses as 'a white object like a football in the sky, travelling faster than an aeroplane'. Flour mill worker Sidney Bird of Worksop was walking near Manton Colliery with four friends: 'At first we thought it was a shooting star. It came from the direction of the pit, then suddenly turned towards Worksop College ... one woman alighting from a bus near Woodland Avenue also spotted the object.'

The Team Valley Sighting

On 1 October 1962 four lorry drivers working on the Team Valley Trading Estate at Gateshead, Tyne and Wear, spotted five silver objects flying overhead. Heaton man George Bellerby was one of them, who described what he saw to an *Evening Chronicle* reporter: 'There were about five of them and they looked quite big. They flew in an easterly direction for a few seconds and then disappeared ... I am positive they were not aircraft because of their shape – they were round and a silvery colour.' A spokesman for the nearby RAF Acklington stated they had nothing flying that morning.

Red-glowing Object Over Fraserburgh

A mysterious red object was observed travelling at high speed over Fraserburgh heading in the direction of Banff on Saturday 13 October 1962. Baker's van boy Gerald Retalic (fifteen) of Gallowhill Road, Fraserburgh, spotted the UFO at 6.30 a.m. as he was leaving for work and called his parents outside to see what Gerald described as 'a red object and it seemed to be glowing like a red hot poker'. He thought it was 'round with two humps' but his father, who had served in the RAF for eleven years, was of the opinion that it was more cone shaped, adding: 'It was a massive thing, and it travelled very fast towards Banff. It was clearly defined and was certainly like nothing I have seen before.' The Retalics watched the UFO travel westwards until it disappeared from view. Just a few minutes later Mrs Retalic spotted the object again from the scullery window and called the family. She recalled: 'When it came back the second time it seemed to be stationary for a while above us.'

Baker's van man James Summers also spotted the object, but, oddly, he considered what he saw to be square shaped. Could they all have seen the same object but perceived a different shape? All agreed what they saw was no aircraft; indeed, it was much larger than any aircraft they knew, it made no sound and there was no light showing.

Over the Lakes

Paper mill worker Harold Threkeld (twenty-one) had driven out onto the low fells near Langdale, about half a mile from Elterwater village seeking some holly for Christmas decorations on 19 December 1962.

Parking his van by the roadside, he walked up the fell and became aware of a buzzing noise which he described as 'like a flight of bees only much louder' that seemed to get louder and louder. Looking around to see what could be causing the noise, he glanced skyward and...

> ...saw a huge great thing in the sky, like a disc or saucer upside down. It seemed to be hovering about 700ft up and I watched it for about a minute or so. Then it came down to about 150ft and I must have watched it for a further two minutes. All at once it swished away at a tremendous speed and disappeared in the direction of Wrynose Pass. It must have been about 50ft to 60ft across and was of a metallic bluish colour ... as it shot away I could see the underneath side very clearly. It had three projections rather like the shape of three beer barrels underneath and it went away with a slant I could see a sort of dome on top. There were other projections round the top of the saucer and I could see through the dome and see that there were something like tables and benches inside.

When questioned about his account by a reporter, Mr Threkeld added to his description: 'Underneath the object there were three protuberances, in the centre of which there was a round mirror-like surface. On its upper side there was a transparent dome from which there glowed a radiant blue light. I could see benches or chairs inside. Round its periphery there were slats or fins. Between its periphery and the dome there were what I took to be portholes or windows, three in number. In motion its colour underwent changes, through a deep red to a greenish white.'

Two Flying Saucers Over Norwich

Mr M. A. Mann, who studied theoretical astronomy as a hobby and regularly watched the sky, was out walking with his wife on Rye Avenue when they spotted and watched two flying saucers between 9.40 and 9.45 on 27 December 1962. The UFOs were just above the horizon, made no discernible sound and could be seen clearly moving along a parallel course from west to east for about eight seconds until they were lost from view among the city lights.

'Tyre' in the Northumberland Sky

A large tyre-shaped object was spotted moving across the sky between Rothbury and Whittingham on 8 April 1963. Engineer Peter

Finlay (thirty-six) of Stakeford was driving his van when he spotted the UFO and told Newcastle-upon-Tyne newspaper the *Journal* of 9 April 1963:

> I stopped the van at once, thinking it was a trick of the windscreen... Then I saw that it was moving across the sky, somewhere between 400 and 800 feet up. I reckon it was about two of three miles away. It was black and looked just like a wagon tyre. I was really sweating by this time. I am usually sceptical of these things but this really frightened me. It moved off in a north-westerly direction. There was a bright orange flash as it went off at a tangent. It moved off very fast and left a trail.

Mr Finlay added that two or three minutes later a jet fighter passed over. He later rang RAF Boulmer to report what he had seen and asked if they had seen anything. When approached by the *Journal* the duty officer at the station said, 'I am afraid I cannot comment on this matter.'

Close Call for Lancashire Couple and UFO

Mr Laurie Greenhalgh and his wife Kathie were asleep in bed at their home on Essex Avenue at Heap Bridge near Bury, Lancashire, when shortly after 4 a.m. on Sunday 28 April 1963 their slumbers were disturbed by the sound of an engine approaching. They both went to their bedroom window, which overlooks the avenue, to investigate what could be making such a racket at that time of the morning, so could you imagine how it must have felt for them to look out of the curtains only to see a flying saucer passing directly overhead? Mrs Greenhalgh told a reporter: 'It almost touched the roof and then we saw it swerve away and hover over a partly built house across the road. It stayed there about ten minutes then touched down.' Mr Greenhalgh added, 'The light from the object was amazing. It was the brightest I have ever seen and the noise of the engines was just like a rocket taking off. As it passed our window it illuminated the whole bedroom. All the light seemed to be projected downwards, none above. I got no impression of shape or size because the light was too bright. Another ten minutes or so elapsed before the noise of the engines started up again and faded away in the distance. This time there was no light or anything.' No other residents in the Greenhalgh's avenue came forward to say they saw anything of the UFO, but a number of the residents in nearby streets claimed to have heard the engines too. Later on, the Greenhalghs went over to the spot where the UFO touched down, but no trace of the landing could be found.

Wirral Air Training Corps Cadets Spot UFO

Nine members of 1123 Air Training Corps Squadron spotted a UFO while attending their drill night at their headquarters on Cross Lane, Bebington, in the borough of Wirral on Merseyside at 9.15 p.m. on 21 May 1963. Cadet Warrant Officer Jeffrey Green (twenty) spotted the UFO first and called eight other cadets to witness it. He told the *Liverpool Echo*: 'the object was in the shape of a sphere which had been sliced in two. It was brilliant in colour. I should imagine it was at an altitude of about 50,000 feet. It seemed to hover and then it disappeared very quickly – too fast for it to have been a jet aircraft. As it went from sight it seemed to be climbing in a westerly direction.'

UFO Over Royton

Patricia Townend was returning after a night out with friends to her home on Oldham Road, Royton, at about 12.30 a.m. on Saturday 15 June 1963 when she spotted a dark grey or black oval-shaped object in the night sky, flying from west to east at around the speed of a helicopter. The first impression was that it was a passenger aircraft with none of its curtains closed and the lights shining through at the sides and underneath and 'something above the base spinning round'. They initially thought it might be a plane or a helicopter, but it made no noise whatsoever.

Saucer Over Scotland

Town Councillor John Gallagher was at work at the Whifflet North Junction signal box on 25 July 1963 when he spotted an aircraft heading towards Renfrew. While he was watching the plane a flying saucer came into view at 9.45 a.m. It hovered about 100 feet above the centre of the town, then moved steadily over to the north above the parish church. Looking away for a few seconds to attend to a passing train, when he looked back the UFO had vanished. Mr Gallagher was convinced it must have moved off at a tremendous speed to disappear from view so quickly. He noted the time as 9.56 a.m. On the same day, six people including the doctor's wife, Ruth Scott, her son Simon (ten) and Kenyan university student Ben Oddotte also reported seeing a UFO of a similar description from her garden in Roslyn. Mrs Potts and her children, James (fourteen) and Sheila, also saw a UFO of a similar description from their home on Dockhart Drive, Chermiston, Edinburgh.

Orbs Over Wolverhampton and Malvern

Amid the July and August 1963 mass UFO sightings around Britain, the *Wolverhampton Express and Star* carried the story of a mysterious object over the town. Matters began on 26 July 1963 when police officers went to investigate reports that a flying saucer had been seen circling over Walsall. Telephone messages had been received from two parts of the town that a strange round object, which changed colour from red to blue-white, had been sighted in the sky. The first report came at 11.30 p.m. from Mr E. E. Dunn of Stephenson Avenue, Bloxwich, who had been with Mr M. G. Cope of Priestley Road chatting on the street looking towards Willenhall when they saw 'a big beaming red light flashing on and off'. While they were watching, it remained stationary two or three times for twenty to thirty seconds. At 11.40 p.m. a similar report was received at police headquarters of a UFO circling in the sky over the Bescot area.

The *Worcester Evening News* of 27 July reported a 'brilliant white ball which turned orange before it moved off' being seen by Donald Lloyd and his wife from their bedroom window on St Andrew's Road, Malvern. They had just drawn the curtains and retired for the night when suddenly the room was lit by a brilliant light that shone through them. Getting out of bed to investigate, Donald looked through the curtains and saw the source was a ball-shaped object that was pulsating with a brilliant light. The object was observed to be moving towards Malvern town in an arc. While travelling south-east, the ball turned orange before disappearing. Three-quarters of an hour later, Mr Lloyd saw the light again. It was coming from the Old Hills direction as before, but this time it turned northwards. Climbing at an angle of 45 degrees, the light faded out and nothing more could be seen of it.

On 30 July, Mr K. C. Martin of Tipton spotted the flashing red light over Stone Cross. As he watched it, the UFO moved very slowly in one direction then came back to the same position again over the Patent Shaft Works. The UFO lingered there, then eventually moved off and disappeared behind a row of houses. Although he observed the light for some time, he could never quite discern the shape behind the red light. Hobbyist astronomer Nigel Neale of Ruskin Avenue, Lanesfield, Wolverhampton, first saw the light over Walsall and Wolverhampton at 11.35 p.m. and observed it with a 1-inch telescope for about thirty minutes until it disappeared. Nigel recounted: 'The object was winking once every three seconds and appeared a brilliant red. When observed with a telescope the UFO was found to consist of four lights.' He did not believe the object to be an aircraft because of its phenomenal speed and twisted path.

At 11.30 p.m. on 1 August, the mystery object with the red flashing light was spotted again. Mrs G. Fradgley of Wallows Road, Brockmoor, spotted it from her bedroom window as it circled over the Wolverhampton area: 'I could not hear it and it did not appear to have any definite shape – it was just a big red light. It circled round for some time and it came towards our house and passed over after about ten minutes.' The UFO disappeared out of sight while travelling in the direction of Quarry Bank.

Triangle Over Kent and the Home Counties

The headlines on the *Chatham, Rochester and Gillingham News* posed the question: 'What was the object that hung for two hours in the sky over Gillingham on Wednesday night?' Numerous witnesses on the evening of 31 July 1963 described the same V-shaped or triangular UFO, which appeared to shine in the sunlight and had a red glow at the bottom. One of the witnesses was David Bird (twenty-four), who came out onto Gardner Street, Gillingham, with several of his neighbours to look at the UFO. He told a reporter: 'I looked out of the window and saw some jet streams and this thing in the sky. It was like a shining white light...It went from a 'V' to a circular shape while it hung in the air.' With only opera glasses to hand, he was able to observe a red glow on the bottom. The object had remained static high in the sky above the town for two hours from around 7.30 p.m. The Air Ministry was approached and a spokesman confirmed the object had been 'seen by people over a wide area of the South-East' and that they were looking into it'. The article offered the following closing remarks: 'It has been suggested it [the UFO] could have been one of the many varieties of meteorological balloons, or a radio-soude balloon.'

The Daily Sketch of 2 August 1963 spoke of a wider 'wave' of sightings: 'For the second night in succession, scores of people telephoned the Air Ministry and the BBC to report a mysterious triangular-shaped object in the sky over London and the Home Counties ... Callers to the Ministry were mainly from Hertfordshire. A spokesman said they could give no explanation.'

The Wimbledon Common Landing

The *Wandsworth Borough News* of 16 August 1963 published an appeal from David Briggs, the area investigator for the British UFO Association, for a woman who had witnessed a UFO landing on Wimbledon Common to contact him, or indeed anyone who had information on it. Mr Briggs had been told by a police constable who had been on patrol on the common that some weeks previously a woman in a distressed state had reported to him that she had seen a UFO, which she described as being as big as 'a double decker bus', land on the common at about 2 a.m. The constable had asked her what she was doing out at that time of the morning, and she had told him that she had been unable to sleep and had decided to take a short walk. After her experience the constable suggested she should return home and go to bed. He then went to investigate the area where the landing was claimed to have taken place but found nothing untoward. Unfortunately, he did not take her name and address. Investigations by Mr Briggs revealed the woman seemed to have been the only person to actually witness the landing, but several other people had seen an object over Wimbledon Common on the same morning.

Return of the Red-orange-glowing UFO

Clearly the glowing object or objects over Kent and London were not over by August. A mysterious object with an orange-red glow was spotted over a number of towns along the Kent coast during September 1963. Believed to have been first reported by Mr Taffy Rooke of Margate, it was followed a few days later with sightings over Ramsgate and another over Herne Bay. Each time the UFO was spotted it appeared to hover a few hundred feet over the town where it was spotted before zipping off over the sea. When approached for comment, RAF Manston stated they 'had no idea what the object can be'.

The Shilbottle Crescent

When driving home from Leicester during the early hours of 15 September 1963, Mrs Joan Allinson of Rosedale Lodge, Alnmouth, Northumberland, and her father were approaching Shilbottle at 3.30 a.m. when their attention was drawn to a golden object, which they estimated to be about 24 feet long hovering at an altitude of 1,000 feet. This object, which Mrs Allison described as being crescent shaped with a golden halo all around it, appeared to follow side of the car for the next thirteen minutes. Disturbingly, the object would suddenly dart towards the car, stop and then speed off in the reverse direction, then sometimes travelled ahead. Mrs Allinson wanted to stop but her father urged her to carry on driving. Mrs Allinson had been terrified and admitted it took her a week to recover from the shock of what she had experienced.

Saucer Over Runcorn

Dick Newby was enjoying a quiet evening at home with his family on Boston Avenue, Runcorn, Halton, Cheshire, on Tuesday 12 November 1963. Mr Newby picks up the story of what happened at about 7.40 p.m.:

> My wife and I were settling down to watch 'Emergency Ward 10', the curtains were open and the lights in the sitting room were off. Then a vivid, bluish-coloured light appeared above the field between my house and Halton and barely a second later a huge star-like thing went sailing across. This, which I believe to be a flying saucer, flew just above the rooftops all the time. My wife was very scared and my fifteen-year-old daughter Ann refused to sleep on her own after seeing the 'thing'. When Ann went to school the next day, two of her friends also said they had seen the peculiar light. I served for seven years in the RAF and I have heard pilots speak about these flying saucers after returning from operations. I myself was very alarmed. I've seen plenty of shooting stars and airliners – but this was neither. After passing over Boston Avenue at chimney pot height the UFO burned a lurid path over the ruins of Halton Castle and disappeared.

Southport Restaurateur and Taxi Driver Followed by a UFO

Mr Softley, the proprietor of L'Avenue restaurant in Southport, was driving from Preston in the early hours of 13 November 1963 when he first saw the saucer: 'I thought at first that it was just a bright star but then I noticed that it was changing course. It seemed to be following us. After a while it changed from white to green. I was quite frightened. After about half an hour the first light was joined by another. They came in quite close as though they were following us. We could see a ring which seemed to be spinning very fast around them.'

Mr Softley pulled into a garage where the police, RAF and coastguards were alerted to what had been seen. Another six people at the garage, including a taxi driver, also saw the lights.

Mt Softley concluded: 'We watched them at the garage for about one hour and then one followed me home and one followed a taxi driver. It was as though they were attracted by the headlights of the cars.'

On the same night 'bright star-like lights' were spotted in the sky at 3 a.m. by passengers leaving the all-night bus at the Fairfield Road and Ashton Old Road stages, High Openshaw, Manchester. Other people in nearby Vine Street and Abbey Hey Lane also spotted the mysterious lights. Witnesses said the lights were 'many times more brilliant than the white and red indicators on an aircraft'. They were observed to move over Reddish, Denton and Hyde then turned north-west where they flew until out of sight.

The Hythe Mothman

The Mothman, a humanoid creature that has entered into modern West Virginian folklore, was reportedly seen in the Point Pleasant area from 15 November 1966 to 15 December 1967 and was later popularised by John Keel in his book *The Mothman Prophecies* (1975). Four years earlier than the American 'Mothman' sighting, on the night of 16 November 1963, teenagers Jenny Holloway (sixteen), Mervyn Hutchinson (eighteen), John Flaxton (seventeen) and another unnamed friend were walking in the Sandling Park area near Hythe, Kent. John Flaxton casually looked at the sky as they walked along and, as he did so, he noticed one of the stars above the woods at Slaybrook Corner seemed to be moving and soon appeared to be descending, at speed, towards the group of friends.

Flaxton told a reporter: 'It was uncanny. The reddish-yellow light was coming out of the sky at an angle of 60 degrees. As it came towards the ground it seemed to hover more slowly. I grew cold all over as it vanished behind a clump of trees.' Suddenly, a bright golden light appeared to be floating about 10 feet above the ground around 200 feet away in the field alongside them.

Flaxton recalled: 'It seemed to move along with us, stopping when we stopped as if it was observing us. The light was oval, about 15 to 20 feet across with a bright, solid core. It disappeared behind trees and a few seconds later a dark figure shambled out. It was all black, about the size of a human but without a head. It seemed to have wings like a bat on either side and came stumbling towards us.'

Mervyn Hutchinson was the member of the group who seemed to have the best view of the figure and was able to add: 'It was just like a bat with webbed feet and no head.' What they were witnessing was beyond their comprehension. Terror-stricken, the teenagers fled the scene.

A few days later, on 21 November, apprentice electrical engineer Keith Croucher (seventeen) was walking past the Brockhill School football pitch that leads to the Sandling estate when he felt a freezing-cold gust of wind and saw 'what looked like a golden mist beginning to cross the pitch. At the centre of the mist was a solid oval light that seemed to move slowly over the ground. The whole thing was about 20 feet square'. Keith was also frightened by what he saw and ran off. He returned a short while later, but the mist and light were both gone.

John McGoldrick (sixteen) heard of Keith Croucher's experience and set off with a friend to Sandlingwoods to investigate. He would later report: 'In a clearing in the woods we found a vast expanse of bracken that had been completely flattened – as if some huge and heavy object had rested there. Nearby we found three giant footprints, almost two feet long and about nine inches across. They must have been a full inch deep.'

McGoldrick returned to the site on 11 December with two reporters and they found the wood lit up by a strange pulsating light: 'It seemed to come from the heart of the trees. We kept watch at a distance for over half and hour but saw nothing except the light. We were far too frightened to go any closer.'

An experience by retired civil servant William Waite (who had worked for the Aeronautical Inspection Board) that he only revealed after these incidents may provide something of a prequel to them. Mr Waite had been walking his dog in the neighbourhood about a week before when: 'I saw this bright bluish-white light, about the size of a gold ball flying directly ahead of me. It travelled quite slowly in a steady horizontal direction. It definitely was not an aeroplane. The whole thing struck me as very peculiar. The light appeared from the north, crossed Sandling Road ... and headed out to sea.'

The local, national and even international press covered the stories and soon explanations were offered such as poachers' torches, magnesium flares and even tales of Slaybrook Corner being haunted and the strange sights being explained as 'ghost lights' or Will-o'-the-Wisp.

When local rector Revd Eric Stanton was asked what he made of it by a reporter, he firmly replied: 'It definitely is not a hoax. Several youngsters have told me about the strange things they have seen. All were very frightened. Obviously they have seen something out of their normal experience.'

Be it an alien, cryptid or a paranormal manifestation, the *Kentish Express* of 29 November 1963 reported: 'Talk of the ghost has reached such a height in the village that parties are being organised to lie in wait. But the women of the village are not so keen on the idea. "I lock and bar the doors and windows as soon as it begins to gets dark," said a housewife.'

UFO Landing at RAF Cosford

Between 11.30 p.m. and just after midnight on 10/11 December 1963, two apprentices at the RAF Technical Training Establishment at Cosford in Shropshire were outside looking across the airfield. Suddenly, a bright, glowing, dome-shaped object swept down from the sky and either landed or hovered behind a hangar used to house Chipmunk training aircraft. Both apprentices could only see the top of the craft or its glow as it lingered there. Shortly afterwards the UFO emitted a green beam of light which swept around like a searchlight. The apprentices watched dumbfounded for about two minutes before dashing off to alert the duty officer, but by the time that they managed to do so the object had disappeared. It was also claimed that a British Railways signalman had also witnessed the UFO from his box.

Upon hearing about the incident, Stafford-based UFO investigator Wilf Daniels drove down to investigate. In his report that he submitted to *Flying Saucer Review* he related how he had chanced upon the chaplain for RAF Cosford while on Albrighton High Street on 9 January 1964 and engaged him in conversation about the incident. Asking if the chaplain knew the two concerned, he confirmed that he did, adding: I've talked about it to them and they really believe they saw it.' Daniels then asked how did they described it, to which the chaplain replied: 'They said it looked like what you would take for a flying saucer...it was down on the ground ... as they watched a trapdoor in the upper part slowly opened. It was then they ran.' When the apprentices reported what they saw 'they were told to sober up but they were not drunk and are quite sane and sensible'.

When approached for comment about the incident the Air Ministry attempted to quash the story, claiming that the two young apprentices had not been sober and that the whole thing was some Christmas prank. The apprentices who witnessed the incident were never named in the press. Subsequently, when the signalman was approached about what he had witnessed he claimed he had seen nothing at all, and the station chaplain would deny the story Wilf Daniels claimed he had told him during their chance meeting. When *Flying Saucer Review* contacted Cosford and spoke to a Flight Lieutenant Stevens, despite reiterating nothing had happened, the apprentices had been drunk and at best they had mistaken the smoke and fire from a passing steam train for a UFO or at worst had just indulged in a hoax. Stevens did, however, admit that an investigation had taken place behind a hangar.

UFO Debris at Penkridge

Early in 1964 Third Class Petty Officer S. M. Branigan, who was attached to US military intelligence, was serving on a tank-landing ship in the Caribbean. He was tasked with the interception of Soviet military transmissions. One message he intercepted and decoded would stun his superiors. The message claimed Russian RADAR had detected and tracked a UFO until it suddenly disintegrated into two sections and fell to earth. The smaller section landed in West Germany and the larger section landed in a rural field near the by-road known as Cocksparrow Lane at Penkridge in Cannock, south Staffordshire.

In 1996 renowned ufologist Nick Redfern tracked down van driver Mr Harold Smith of Bloxwich, who claimed he had seen a 'delta-shaped object' partially covered by a tarpaulin in the field at Penkridge and saw it being lifted onto an aircraft transporter. He claimed he had also taken photographs but was later stopped at a roadblock manned by police, army and RAF. His camera was confiscated and when it was eventually returned to him, he found the film had been removed. According to Redfern, between his telephone call to arrange the interview and arrival Mr South had been telephoned by a military or government official, warning him not to talk to Redfern. This had clearly worried the man, who felt he could say nothing more about what he had witnessed.

A retrospective article in the *Shropshire Star* by Mike Lockley in February 2023 stated the Penkridge wreckage was recovered in an operation involving NATO and the USAF. The crash portion that was recovered was shipped to Wright Patterson Air Force base in Dayton, Ohio; some fragments were even believed to have been sent to the British Defence Science and Technology Laboratory at Porton Down in Salisbury, Wiltshire.

A 2023 FOI request submitted to the MOD requesting disclosure about the incident received a reply from Air Command Secretariat, which stated: 'A search for the information has now been completed within the Ministry of Defence, and I can confirm that no information in scope of your request is held.' It went on to point out: 'You may wish to be aware that the MOD has no opinion on the existence of either extraterrestrials, Unidentified Flying Objects (UFO) or Unidentified Aerial Phenomena (UAP).'

'Little Green Men' at Felling

When dealing with reports of UFOs, it pays to be sceptical but keep an open mind. Sometimes one genuine incident can attract so much local and even national attention that other people come forward with their stories of what they saw. The problem then can be in deciding whether they were genuine witnesses, delusional or just those who wanted to be in the limelight. In June 1964 it was claimed by several residents of the Leam Lane estate in Felling, County Durham, that three egg-shaped UFOs had been spotted in the sky above the area. According to some witnesses, one of these had even landed nearby and some of its occupants had been spotted on the ground.

The centre of activity was Hopedene Avenue where several residents claimed to have heard a strange buzzing noise. Keith Bell (thirteen) claimed he was looking out of one of the windows of his family home and saw a terrific flash in the sky 'then a flying saucer, egg-shaped and giving off a bright glow appeared'. Keith's mother refused to believe him until she saw the flashes herself which lit up the whole front room. Then there was David Wilson (fourteen) who claimed he has seen 'several small green creatures, about 2 feet high running around a haystack on a farm near the estate'.

The Tyneside UFO Society sent a full field-survey team to investigate and interview witnesses. TUFOS secretary Mr J. Leslie Otley commented: 'While we appreciate that this thing has snowballed until there is a vein of pure fantasy we nevertheless believe that these lights and the humming sound heard by so many people are somehow connected. Our investigators have found that many sensible people have heard this noise and that young David Wilson is described by his parents and friends as a truthful boy who would not invent anything of this nature.'

TUFOS's field investigation co-ordinator Bill Muir (who would, with his friend Miss Lambton, see an oval orange-white disc flying over Washington, County Durham, on 12 July 1964) subsequently commented: 'There were so many people involved in this that there must have been a lot in what they had to say.' And of the story of the aliens by the haystack: 'We took that part of the story with a pinch of salt at first but just one month later, there was a report of more "green men" in Liverpool. Their descriptions tallied remarkably so we have taken the whole episode quite seriously ever since.'

Perhaps unconnected, but it is nevertheless interesting to note that later that same month Edwin Vipond and his wife, Eileen, who kept the Moor House Inn at Seaton Burn in the neighbouring county of Northumberland, also spotted a similar UFO. The couple were asleep in bed on the warm night of Friday 26 June with their window open. At around 2 a.m. the couple were awakened by a strange sound. Mrs Vipond takes up the story: 'We heard this loud buzzing noise like the high-pitched buzzing of a spinning top. It kept droning on and on until I went to the window to see what was causing it ... I looked up and there high in the sky was the saucer ringed in an electric blue light. The whole saucer seemed to be pulsing up and down.'

Mr Vipond joined his wife at the window and saw the same thing, adding: 'I could hardly believe my eyes. The saucer was moving in an east to west direction. Then it shot upwards and out of sight.' Two nights later, Mrs M. E. Godfrey of Wingrove Avenue, Newcastle, spotted 'a brilliantly lit circular object in a very clear sky for 5 minutes drifting from south to north. The upper part had a bluish tinge while the lower part was much brighter.'

The Penshaw Portal?

The Penshaw Monument, built between 1844 and 1845 to commemorate John Lambton, 1st Earl of Durham (1792–1840), is a superb 70-foot-tall structure built in the style of a Greek temple on the top of Penshaw Hill, Sunderland. It is visible for miles around and it certainly has an air of mystery about it, having been the scene of several UFO sightings over the years. There is a possibility the sky above might a portal, which Mrs Margaret Haw might have seen in action in 1964. At 9.45 p.m. on 1 July 1964, Mrs Haw was watching the summer sunset over Penshaw when she saw something strange: 'A thin grey line appeared in an orange sunset. Gradually, it grew thicker and changed colour to dark grey. Clouds were moving around it but the object was quite still. Two aeroplanes appeared and began circling. The UFO then faded away slowly. It reappeared after a few minutes and was watched for 3 minutes before it finally disappeared.'

The Otterburn Lights

In 1964, Chief Observer Robert Telfer of Elsdon had been a member of the Northumberland Royal Observer Corps for over twenty years and knew the skies above him well. However both he and members of his team of observers at their Otterburn post began to observe mysterious 'lights' performing what would be astounding feats for any known aircraft over the Otterburn Moors on numerous occasions. Mr Telfer told a reporter: 'They [the lights] always seem to appear to the north-east of Elsdon and they have a set pattern. Sometimes they are still and then they streak off at fantastic speeds then disappear. I have noticed one light by itself and then a number together.' He did point out that the objects were too high up for him to recognise any shape they may have.

'We don't know what they are but they are certainly there and we are confident they are no known kind of aircraft.'

Mr Telfer was not alone in his sightings. Local school teacher Joseph McKie, a member of the British Astronomical Society, had also noticed the lights and he too was baffled: 'One theory is these bodies are scanning discs from flying saucers. I wouldn't know about that, but as far as I know no such phenomena are listed in any standard works and I have seen nothing like them before.'

The lights continued to reappear and, unable to explain what he had been seeing, Mr Elsdon compiled a special report on the matter which he submitted to the MOD in 1967. There is no record of their response.

UFO Chased by Jets Over Newcastle

At 5.35 p.m. on 2 October 1964, Mr T. Hastings spotted a silver metallic object hovering in the sky 'very high up but clearly visible with the naked eye' not far from his home in the Newcastle suburb of Heaton. He watched the object for about five minutes until 'two jets appeared and closed in on the UFO. When the planes got close to the UFO moved off in a west direction. The planes tried to intercept it but the UFO accelerated and lost them.' Later that same month, on 22 October, Mr J. Dunbar of Rothbury Terrace, Heaton, and Miss P. Dorkin of Newcastle also spotted what he described as 'a silver sphere, as bright as Venus but two and a half times its size, moved down towards earth then cut off at right angles maintaining a constant speed. Then it disappeared into a cloud near the moon.'

Red Saucer Over Newcastle

On 6 November 1964 Mr S. Kerrison (twenty-six) of Beaumont Street, Newcastle, a head messenger for British Railways, was walking down to the Newcastle Forth Bank at about 5.50 p.m. when he looked up into the sky over Gateshead and saw a red object in a stationary position. He noted: 'The top of the object glowed orange-red and the other half a brighter red. When I looked 2 minutes later it had disappeared.'

The Warminster 'Thing'

From the mid-1960s and throughout the 1970s the historic town of Warminster, Wiltshire, on the fringe of Salisbury Plain and its army training centres, became a mecca for flying saucer spotting, with groups regularly gathering on local hillsides to watch the skies all year round. It all came as quite a shock to the little town of 11,000 souls.

The story begins on 24/25 December 1964 when people across Warminster heard a terrible sound in the sky. Head postmaster Roger Rump was awoken from his sleep by what sounded like every tile being ripped from the roof of his house late on the night of 24 December. At around 6.12 a.m. on Christmas Day 1964 local woman Mrs Marjorie Bye was on her way to Holy Communion when she appeared to suffer the brunt of the sonic pressure waves when she heard strange 'crackling noises' in the sky above her and suddenly sonic shockwaves pounded her head, neck and shoulders from above. She was left with her senses skewed and her legs almost too weak to carry her to her church.

Others heard it too. Even at nearby Knook Camp at Heytesbury, soldiers of 1st Battalion, the Welch Regiment, also heard the sound; the guards were stood in anticipation of being required to respond to whatever had generated the noise. A sergeant at the camp described the sound 'as if a huge chimney stack from the main block was ripped from the rooftop, then scattered in solid chunks of masonry across the whole camp area'.

In February 1965, a flock of pigeons were killed in flight and landed on a woodland clearing on the Longleat estate, owned by the Marquess of Bath. Two witnesses who examined the birds shortly afterwards were convinced that rigor mortis had almost immediately set in. Crockerton resident David C. Holton, a surgical chiropodist and keen naturalist, was alerted to what had happened by a neighbour who claimed he had 'heard a roaring sound while walking in the woods and saw dozens of pigeons in normal flight suddenly fall to the ground'. Holton went to the site and examined the birds after they came to ground. Having ruled out every other natural explanation, he was left with the opinion that sonic shockwaves, like those experienced the previous December, had wiped out the flock.

Then came the first sighting of the UFO many would attribute the sound waves to. Mrs Hilda Hebdidge (sixty-three) spotted a cigar-shaped object 'covered with bright lights that remained stationary and winked and blinked' above Warminster until they gradually faded away in the sky on 19 May 1965.

During the first week in June a 'brightly glowing cigar-shaped object' many would soon refer to simply as 'The Thing' made another appearance over Warminster. Mrs Patricia Phillips, wife of Revd P. Graham Phillips, the vicar of Heytesbury, and her three children were among those who reported seeing it at a little after 9 p.m. on 3 June 1965. She recalled how her son Nigel (thirteen) had spotted the UFO first: 'He rushed outside with his telescope but when we went out we could see it clearly with the naked eye. It was a pale yellow light but bright against a clear sky … It was elongated and extremely high up. It stayed quite still for about 30 minutes and then seemed to contract and gradually disappeared.' There was no sound emitted when they saw it. Others spotted it too, including hospital physiotherapist Penelope Long and seventeen people who had been fishing or swimming at Bath's Lake, Shearwater.

Other strange objects were also seen in the sky over the following months, including what were described as 'twin red hot pokers in the sky with a red ball of fire around it'. They were spotted by retired factory security guard Harold Horlock and his wife, Dora, from the back door of their home in Warminster as they let out their cat, Tinker, at 3.45 a.m. on 17 August 1965. It seems that Tinker was also aware of the odd presence in the sky as they ran under a bush and hid there in terror until the UFO disappeared.

By this time the *Warminster Journal* was being inundated with letters from people who had also seen 'The Thing' or heard unnaturally thunderous noises and experienced sonic shockwaves themselves. It was not long before the stories were picked up by national and international newspapers. Interest was heightened further still when a public meeting to enquire into the phenomena with council chairman Emlyn Rees presiding was held on the August bank holiday. It was one of the best-attended meetings the town had ever known, with 200 people crammed into the assembly room and an estimated 300 more sat outside on the stone steps to listen as best they could to the proceedings inside.

Those who were known to have sighted the UFOs over the town were soon besieged by reporters, and the story heightened further still when holidaymakers believed they saw extraterrestrial beings when exploring the surrounding countryside. But it would be a photograph taken by factory worker Gordon Faulkner (twenty-three) from the front doorstep of his home with his Halina 35-mm camera of a flying saucer at 8.20 p.m. on Sunday 29 August 1965 that really set the media alight. Gordon described how he had taken the photo to Arthur Shuttlewood, editor of the *Warminster Journal*.

Gordon had been setting off to visit his mother and had the camera with him because he seldom used it and his sister wished to borrow it. As he shut his front door behind him, he turned around and there was a UFO in the sky over Warminster. He recalled: 'It was a silvery object, Not at all that height … as it flew past over the south of the town. I could just make out the unusual shape. It was circular … it was soundless – not a whisper of noise. Hurriedly I got my camera free and aimed. The line of flight was so fast it was impossible to follow. So I held the camera well in front of it and pressed the trigger as it entered the view-finder. I didn't dream I'd get anything on film at all. It shook me rigid when I saw what came out.'

Never seeking a penny for the image, Gordon passed the print to Shuttlewood fully expecting him to scoff at it, but that is far from what happened. The story hit the pages of the *Daily Mirror* on Friday 10 September 1965 under the headline of 'The Thing ... a strange story of the goings on in the skies above an English country town'. And the photograph itself was published in the same paper along with a follow-up article the following day in which Percy Carr, the vice-chairman of Warminster Chamber of Commerce, was quoted after seeing the photo and in the knowledge of the many UFO sightings over the town: 'We have something that I'm sure will become more notorious than the Loch Ness monster.' He was not far wrong.

To cap off these incidents, on 12 September 1965 papers carried the story of Second World War veteran Major Bill Hill, the Commanding officer of 4th Battalion Wiltshire Regiment (Warminster and Westbury) TA, who was driving to a drill night round a bend at Calloway Clumo near Warminster when his car 'started jumping and jolting up and down violently with its wheels leaving the ground'. Major Hill wondered if his car was overheating, but when he got out, popped the bonnet and checked the radiator it was at a normal temperature. Major Hill, however, 'sensed something fantastic and oddly sinister in the air. It was like the sounds – magnified thousands of times at least – of high-powered refrigerating or deep-freeze units. But this was way, way above that. The vibrations grew less and the car gently swayed, instead of jumping about madly. After three minutes it had disappeared entirely. I pressed the starter button of my car and it purred away perfectly'. The major had his car fully checked over the following day, but there were no issues discovered that could have caused the juddering halt of the previous night. Could it be the sonic pressure waves of the UFO had struck again?

After the press coverage of the photo and the stories of UFO activity in Warminster, the town's hotels and guesthouses were soon packed out by those keen to see the mysterious objects over the town for themselves. A host of newspaper articles, tv reports, magazine features and books appeared over the ensuing months and years about the phenomena, and there were regular sightings of UFOs over Warminster. By far the most engaging of all of these were the books such as *The Warminster Mystery*

(1967), *The Flying Saucerers* (1976) and *UFO Magic in Motion* (1979) written by Arthur Shuttlewood.

Rather like bird watchers, many would come from across the country with friends to spend weekend breaks and summer holidays at Warminster armed with binoculars and cameras. Nearby Cradle Hill became a popular place for UFO spotters to gather and they were frequently rewarded with sightings of various unexplained lights and objects in the sky above them, which kept the interest alive over subsequent years. Visitors may well have also visited the Fountain Centre, read *The Fountain Journal* which charted UFO sightings or stayed at Star House, which was run by Peter and Jane Paget, with Jane's mother Margaret specifically catering for those seeking a glimpse of UFOs. Peter Paget would publish his excellent *UFO-UK* book in 1980. Sadly, the interest in UFOs at Warminster has faded away, and Star House, the Fountain Centre and *Fountain Journal* are no longer running. Arthur Shuttlewood died in Warminster in 1996 and is sadly missed, but mysterious objects and lights are still to be seen in the skies above the town.

Football Match Spectators See UFO

Many of the spectators at the pre-season trial football match of Carlisle vs Bury on 13 August 1965 spotted a UFO in the sky above the stands and pitch. Mr D. Hutton informed *Flying Saucer Review* that the object had appeared between 8.40 and 9.20 p.m. and it was 'brilliant white, about fifty per cent brighter than Venus' hanging in the sky over the South West. The following day Mr Hutton was playing cricket in West Cumberland and, much to his surprise, found many people in Whitehaven and Cockermouth had also seen the same object.

UFO Over Westmorland Pennines

The Yorkshire Post and a number of national papers including *The Guardian* and *Daily Express* covered the account of a UFO sighting by Miss Katherine Chambers who was staying with a group of friends in Windmore Green, Appleby, in the Westmorland Pennies on 15 August 1965:

> My friends and I had gone to bed, and had been talking a while when I heard a sheep making a most peculiar noise [a local farmer would also confirm his cattle and sheep had been restive and made a lot of noise during the night]. My friends took little heed but when we also heard cattle moaning we really took notice ... My bed was directly under

> the window and despite my friends protests I knelt up and looked out. The first thing I saw, directly ahead, was a pair of vivid orange lights flashing in the sky. I shouted to my friends to hurry, and, their curiosity overcoming their fear, they joined me.

Katherine kept the object under observation from about midnight until 1.15 a.m. on 15 August. The sky was clear and moonlit. Katherine's account continues:

> As my eyes became accustomed to the light I could see a dark shape connecting the orange lights. More frightened than ever, my friends went back to bed, but I continued to watch as the object seemed to move slowly backwards and forwards in the sky and changed from a horizontal to a vertical position, with the lights flashing intermittently. For a short while it seemed to disappear, but returned, this time in a beam of light rather like that of a searchlight from the ground. The object was in the widest part of the beam.

Katherine began to feel quite ill, drained and tired, so she returned to her bed. She recalled: 'The object was still there but only the lights seemed to be visible by that time. The rest seemed to have blended into the sky. All the time there was a low whirring sound.' When reproduced in *Flying Saucer Review* it was accompanied by the comments:

> The object was described as being at first sighting 'clear and distinct'. There were no sparks or smoke. A rough estimate of its length was 50ft but its size was also compared to that of a golf ball held at arm's length. This could indicate a very large object when one considered that two Moons' widths are covered by a sixpence held at arm's length. It also occurs to us that the light beam could have come from the object, in which case it was being focussed on to the ground beneath.

Flying Saucers Over Stonehenge

Over the years numerous ancient sites around Britain and the world have become known for regular sightings of UFOs above them. Could this be that because of the high volume of visitors to these sites there is an increased likelihood of UFO observation? Or is it, perhaps, that some visitors will expect to see or experience something so ardently that they believe they witness something odd in the sky? Or could there really be a portal for UFOs above Stonehenge that had been known and venerated by the ancient peoples of Britain?

One sighting among many was when Southend-on-Sea residents Mr and Mrs P. Willsher were driving past Stonehenge in August 1965, when Mrs Willsher saw: 'Four silvery objects coming over a hill.' At first she wondered if they were sunrays catching the wings of an aeroplane, but there was no sound in the sky above. She drew her husband's attention to what she was seeing. Mr Willsher pulled over to the side of the road, stopped the car, got out and looked up, recalling: 'At first I could see only two of these queer things ... then a third emerged and a fourth joined the trio shortly after. They were moving circular discs.'

Red Sphere Over Jarrow

At 10.30 p.m. on the evening of 26 August 1965 some twenty people on Inverness Road, Jarrow, all witnessed a red-glowing spherical object (which had the red fading to orange towards the periphery of the craft) flying from south to north at an angle of elevation of 90–45 degrees. Further reports revealed the object had been seen flying very fast and high over the town by various witnesses a total of eight times in a three-hour period.

Cigar-shaped UFO Over Ryton

At 8.30 p.m. on 1 September 1965 Mr and Mrs R. J. Holmes and their son Mr Kimberley Holmes (a civil servant) of Greenside, Ryton, County Durham, and his friend Miss P. A. Forster spotted a cigar-shaped object in the sky and watched it for approximately twenty minutes. Mr Holmes reported the incident to Tyneside UFO Society, who despatched Harry Lord to take a statement from the witnesses of what they saw.

The sky was blue with streaky clouds and a sunset. They were looking westward over Cumberland when they first saw the cigar-shaped object at an elevation of 45 degrees. Estimated to have been about 100 feet up in the air, it looked to be about 1 inch long when viewed from the ground. It was black when first spotted but seemed to be able to change its colour to red or silver. It also had red lights, one on either side towards the front and three at the rear that were all 'flashing furiously'. There was no sound. It was about six times larger than a star. It was very bright and moved slowly, hovering at times, and it disappeared as suddenly as it had appeared. Three more independent witnesses – one of them another resident of Ryton and two more from nearby Crawcrook – also saw the same UFO.

UFO Passes Over Poole

On the night of 10/11 September 1965 at approximately 00.25 a.m. Mr A. E. Harvey of Curlieu Road in Oakdale, Poole, in Dorset had just locked up his garden shed for the night. Looking up into the night sky, he spotted a curious blue light moving from east to south-west which he estimated to be at 5,000 feet. As the UFO came closer, Mr Harvey observed a ring of red spots or lights around its centre. It was revolving in an anti-clockwise direction. In view for approximately four minutes as it passed overhead, it was seen to have a blue/white outer edge, a bright red centre and a dark ring separating them. It emitted a sound like a compressed air leak on a garage air line.

The Langenhoe Incident

On 14 September 1965 engineer Paul Green (twenty-nine) was considerably shaken by his encounter with a UFO. He was interviewed by Dr Bernard Finch and a verbatim account was reproduced in *Flying Saucer Review* shortly afterwards:

> It was about 1.00am on Sunday 14 September that I first saw the 'thing'. It was a bright clear night, the moon was up and I could see the stars twinkling overhead. I was returning to my home in West Mersea, having visited my fiancee in Colchester. I had had nothing to drink and was feeling very fit. I was travelling on a motorbike and averaging 40 miles per hour. Just before reaching Pete Tye common a few yards south of Langenhoe, I overtook a motor scooter. My bike was purring along, the engine sounding a healthy note.
>
> As I approached the straight road south to Langenhoe Hall I heard a high-pitched humming over to my left (the east). This noise became louder and I looked up for the sign of an approaching aircraft. I could see none but noticed a small pinpoint of blue light to the east over Brightlingsea (about 5 miles away). The light was winking and became rapidly larger, and I then realised that it was coming in my direction from over Langenhoe Marsh. The humming then became very much louder and changed to a high-pitched buzz.
>
> It dawned on me that the light and the sound were connected. The engine of my bike then began to cough and splutter; it missed several times and then stopped dead and the lights went out. The blue flashing light was now about a mile away to the east. I could make out some sort of an outline and an enormous object spun into view, looming up large and uncanny out of the sky. It resembled the upper

half of a large spinning top and was about the size of a gasometer. There appeared to be a dome on top, inside of which there was flashing a strange blue light. The object slowly descended, tilting as it did so, and I was able to catch a glimpse of its under belly. This was rimmed by numerous round objects, the whole resembling a 'ball race'.

I had dismounted and approached towards the object. I felt spellbound and was not able to move or speak, just as if I had become paralysed. The flashing blue light became so intense that it was painful, and it appeared to fluctuate in rhythm with my heartbeat and hit against my chest. I felt myself tingling all over rather like the electric shock one gets when handling an electrified cattle fence for too long. The buzzing then became quieter, and the object descended in the area of Wick where there are several farm houses.

Suddenly, the scooter that I had overtaken on the road approached, its engine coughed and stopped, and the rider, a young lad in a leather jacket, dismounted and stood petrified staring at the blue light ... he neither spoke nor looked in my direction. My head began to throb and I felt as if there was a tightening band round it. With a great effort I was able to move and I grasped my bike and tried to start it. I pushed it along the road, and was gratified to hear the engine suddenly burst into life. I mounted and raced as fast as I could away from the dreadful and 'painful' blue light. As I raced down the road the object was hidden by a tall line of hedges on the side of the road but I could still see for some time a blue glow in the sky.

I arrived home at nearly 2.00am ... The following day I noticed that my hair and clothes were crackling in an unusual manner and appeared to be charged with electricity. A few days later I was discussing my experience with a friend who lives at Shrub End which is 5 miles NW of Wick. He told me that at about the same time his dog commenced to bark and as he opened the door to put it out a large blue light passed rapidly in the sky directly overhead towards the North West.

The Terrifying Power of a Suffolk UFO

Geoffrey Maskey was out in his car with friends Mike Johnson and Mavis Forsyth on 20 September 1965. Mr Maskey had parked his car on Walton Avenue in Felixstowe at around 10.30 p.m. and the three were chatting away quite happily when suddenly Mike made a hasty exit from the car without saying where he was going. Geoffrey picks up the story:

I thought this was most peculiar, as he didn't say where he was going. Several minutes passed while we were waiting for him and then suddenly we heard a weird high-pitched humming noise, almost like something from a science-fiction film. Mavis was terrified by the sound. I myself wondered where it was coming from and I looked out of the car window to see an orange-coloured object above the trees approximately 100ft above us. It was oval in shape, apparently 6 feet long and emitting an orange glow. It is difficult to describe it as the lane was lit up by its glow. As the object disappeared behind the trees, the alarming noise was once more heard.

By this time we were wondering what had happened to Mike. I called to him, but he didn't answer, so I reversed the car down the lane and called his name again. Suddenly he emerged from the hedge clutching his neck and eyes, stumbling away from the car. I thought he was having a game with us, but when he collapsed in the road, I went over to him. I found him unconscious. Mavis and I took him to Felixstowe Hospital. At the hospital he came round and in a confused state, mumbled about the noise and the light 'getting' him.

The doctor examined him and told us he had experienced a severe shock. We noticed some burn marks on the back of his neck and I also felt a small bump under the skin just below his right ear. The doctor didn't know what to make of it. Mike was transferred to Ipswich Hospital from where he was discharged. He spoke then of 'a man in flames pointing at him' and stated that some force seemed to have pulled him from the car.

UFO Tracked by Newcastle Airport

At 9.10 p.m. on 21 September 1965 Mr G. Auld, the Duty Controller, Tower Staff and crash crew on duty at Woolsington Airport (now Newcastle International Airport) spotted a very bright UFO surrounded by a white halo which they tracked for some five minutes travelling in a north-east direction. Described as being much bigger than a star, it held a zig-zag course below cloud level, circled, lost height then suddenly increased speed and disappeared.

UFO Over Bridgwater Causes Cattle Stampede

The Yorkshire Post of 26 October 1965 contained a report of a mysterious red light UFO:

A mystery aerial object thought to be a flying saucer has been seen by four anglers on a night fishing trip in Somerset. The men narrowly escaped being trampled to death by a herd of fifty cows that had been terrified by the object. It was like all pandemonium let loose, and we hid behind the car in case the cows should sweep us into the water said Jim Sharman. It happened soon after midnight as the party were fishing in the King's Sedgemoor Drain, Bridgwater.

Mr Sharman (21), a Sheffield coal merchant, said they first noticed something unusual when they saw a red light approaching u the drain. 'It was just like the red light on an aircraft, and as it got nearer it was so bright that it lit up the bank and surrounding fields. The light tapered to the rear, about 12 feet away, and when it got overhead it hovered, flashing on and off.' The anglers shone two spotlights towards the object, but the light was so bright that they could not see where it was coming from. 'It became so bright the cows started making a heck of a noise and chased around the field. After 15 minutes the object suddenly accelerated away and quickly disappeared. 'There was no sound, and we don't know whether it was a flying saucer, space ship or a secret craft from a nearby airfield.'

Policeman Stunned by UFO at Wilmslow

PC Colin Perks (twenty-eight) of Cheshire Constabulary was on duty checking the doors of shops which border the east side of the Alderley Road (A34), Wilmslow, near Manchester, at 4.10 a.m. on Friday 7 January 1966 when he heard an uncanny high-pitched whine. He could only say it was similar in sound to a high-speed electric motor. Turning around to see if he could spot what was making the noise, he looked to the east over the car park behind the shops and the meadow beyond. About 100 yards from PC Perks, he saw a solid-looking object hovering about 35 feet above the grass.

He had a clear and unobstructed view of what appeared to be a flying saucer. It had rounded but fairly sharp changes in the profile of the craft, and a top dome which appeared to be a continuation of the surface. He could not see any openings or windows anywhere on the object. The upper surfaces glowed steadily 'with an eerie greenish-grey colour'. The glow also filled the air around the object but did not alter its clearly defined outline. The base was 'dark, circular, featureless and flat. It was probably horizontal but presented an elliptical outline to his point of view'. PC Perks was of the opinion that the base of the craft was a 30-foot-diameter circle.

Neither the object nor PC Perks moved for five seconds; on reflection he would admit candidly he probably did not move because he had been rendered immobile by fear but insisted he kept his wits about him. PC Perks was left with a slight stammer for a few days after the sighting that he attributed to the fright he had suffered.

After those five seconds the saucer moved rapidly away over the east-south-east, passing near to a leafless tree, over the hedge, crossed a suburban road and disappeared over the roofs of the houses on the far side of the road.

Perks quickly sketched what he had seen and headed to his station to write up a report. He also telephoned Ringway Airport and Jodrell Bank to see if anything of what he had just seen had been reported by anyone else. After the story reached the press Mrs Amy Walker came forward to offer some corroboration having seen 'a pearly green object' over Lindow Garage that was about 50 feet away from her house.

The Conisborough Flying Saucers Photograph

One of the most iconic UFO photographs was taken in Britain by Cadeby Colliery mining apprentice Stephen Pratt (fifteen) shortly after returning with his mother, Therese, to their home at No. 11 Leslie Avenue, Conisborough, Doncaster, South Yorkshire, after popping out for some fish and chips on Monday 28 March 1966. They first noticed a bright orange light which hung motionless in the sky. Therese sent her son in to grab his Kodak Instamatic 50 camera and he snapped the three UFOs looking down Montague Road toward The Crags as the objects sped by at fantastic speed towards Sheffield. Sure enough, the negative showed the three craft and, after being submitted to six months of rigorous examination by photographic experts, including analysis by Kodak, all concluded that the photo was genuine. Stephen always maintained the photograph was taken without any trickery.

Van Driver Affected by UFO Over Sawtry

This case is based on an original report made by Malcolm Bull and John Stear of the Halifax Branch of BUFORA that was reproduced in *Flying Saucer Review*. Van Driver Peter Rushton and Driver's Mate Derek Robinson were asleep in the back of a van they were bringing back from London on 28 April 1966. They had turned off the main Stamford to Lincoln Road to a side road near Sawtry where they had parked up for the night to get some sleep. At around 5 a.m. Mr Rushton woke up with a start, suffering from a horrible acidic taste in his mouth and having great difficulty breathing.

Seeking some fresh air, he moved to the back of the van and pushed up the sliding shutter. Outside the birds were screeching horribly and as he looked to the sky he saw a large, orange spherical object that appeared to be slowly moving away from the back of the vehicle.

Rushton woke his mate up and they both watched as the object stopped moving and hung motionless in the air. They also spotted a second identical object hovering about half a mile away to their left. Both objects appeared to be about the size of a sixpence at arm's length. Suddenly the two objects changed places at incredible speed by moving clockwise along semicircular paths. Both spheres then faded from the sight of the men. As the objects disappeared quiet was restored among the birds and nothing more was seen of the strange orbs. Mr Rushton, who had served nine years in the RAF until May 1965, had never seen anything like it before. He had been quite disturbed by the sighting and relived the incident on several occasions during vivid dreams.

Witness Burned by UFO at Wood Green

Keith Palmer was making his way to his bathroom at his home on Ellenborough Road, Wood Green, in North London, at 2 a.m. on 15 August 1966. Glancing out of the window, he was shocked to see a glowing spherical object in the night sky that was almost half the size of a full moon coming towards Wood Green from the direction of Edmonton. Wondering if he was still dreaming Keith woke his wife up who confirmed he was not seeing things.

The UFO stopped and hovered over an old tree that was around 150 yards from the Palmers' home. They saw it was a large and intensely glowing disc, so bright that no widows, portholes or additional features could be seen. After it had hovered for a while two smaller, brightly illuminated discs emerged from the craft and took up on either side of the main body of the UFO. As soon as the smaller discs were in position it emitted beams which lit up the ground in cones of pure white light. Mr Palmer was able to read the hands of his watch and see the time was 2.10 a.m.

Keith opened the window and leaned out to get a better view. As he did, so the two smaller objects extinguished their lights and flew back into the main craft. Now tilting slightly to one side, the UFO began to slowly move even closer to the house. Mrs Palmer was now very afraid of what was going to happen next.

As the UFO got closer the sheer size of the thing was awe-inspiring and now appeared more pear shaped than spherical as when they had first seen it. Now in close proximity, they heard it making noises similar to a child's humming top and a muffled jet. The object passed over the house, and as it did so Mr Palmer could see a series of coloured lights revolving in a random fashion on the underside of the disc. Once the UFO had passed over it was out of sight and was not seen again by the Palmers.

The following morning however, Mr Palmer noticed a rash on his face similar to sunburn. His wife and son were also suffering from inexplicably painful headaches and sore necks. When the site of the tree and the area around it was investigated by ufologist Colin McCarthy in the immediate aftermath of the Palmers' sighting he found an elderberry bush near the old tree had died in its centre. There appeared to be circular holes in the ground and a large depression with flattened grass. He also took the opportunity to visit the Palmers at their home and found them an intelligent and sincere couple. Mr McCarthy was certainly tempted to speculate that the rash suffered by Mr Palmer after the sighting could have been caused by ultra-violet rays given off by the UFO as it passed over him.

Southampton Z-Car Alerted to UFO

At 9.45 p.m. on 19 September 1966 John Dack was sitting on public bench in Aldermoor, Southampton, when he spotted a strange bright light in the sky over the town that kept giving off purple flashes. He was so concerned by what he was seeing he reported it to Southampton police. A police 'Z-Car' was duly sent to Aldermoor, and sure enough the light was still there. He radioed back: 'There is such an object in the sky to the west...it keeps flashing blue, red and white lights and dropping coloured flares. There is no sound of an engine and it does not appear to be an aircraft.' The object then moved off at high speed towards Eastleigh. Calls to both Southampton Airport and the local weather centre could shed no light on what had been witnessed in the sky that night.

The Pegswood Orb

Ron Martino (twenty-four), an electrician and member of a local beat group of Beaumont Street, Blyth, Northumberland, was walking along a rural stretch of road near Ashington on his way to visit relatives at Pegswood on the night of 13 February 1967. Ron spotted 'a glowing amber ball' in the sky which he pointed out to another man also on the road who dismissed it as an aircraft, but it struck both men as odd that neither of them could hear aircraft engines. Shortly afterwards, the other man turned off the road and Ron was left walking alone. It was then that events really ramped up, as Ron described: 'The light circled round me twice at a distance and the third time stopped in the air straight behind me. It then came straight at me. I was terrified and started running...

When a car came round the corner the light disappeared. It returned after the car had passed. I carried on running and then about six cars came in quick succession and the light disappeared altogether.' By that time he had reached Pegswood, though was quite shaken by his experience. Ron had no idea what it was that he had seen, but he was absolutely certain it was not an aircraft.

The Brixham Dome UFO

At 11.30 a.m. on 28 April 1967 Brixham coastguard Brian Jenkins was alerted to a UFO by a group of workmen at the Berry Head quarry that they had spotted overhead. Jenkins kept the object under observation through binoculars for about an hour as it rose from 1,600 feet when first seen to 16,000 feet and it climbed out of sight. He told a reporter: 'I have never seen anything like it in my life. It was about twice as big as a Vulcan bomber, or if you like a street of houses. It was much too big to be a meteorological balloon.' He described what he saw as 'like a transparent dome with what looked like a door on one side'. He reported the object to the RAF, but by the time a spotter plane had arrived from Plymouth the object had disappeared. The RAF station at Mount Batten stated: 'It can't be one of our weather balloons; you would never see it at 16,000ft.'

The British UFO 'Flap' of Summer 1967

There are some twenty-five meanings listed in the Oxford English Dictionary's entry for the verb 'flap', one of which is a state of worry and excitement. It is rooted in the Second World War when the term became attached to real fears of air attacks, enemy spies landing by parachute or sea and invasion scares. In the years after the Second World War, when so many of those involved in watching our skies and coastline for enemy intruders in war service roles such as the Royal Air Force or Royal Observer Corps witnessed UFOs personally or became involved in the investigation of flying saucers, it was no surprise that the wartime lingo was applied whenever there were a proliferation of sightings, and it would be described as a 'flap'.

Reports of UFOs from across the country hit an all-time high in the British press in 1967. Sightings had been made throughout the year, but matters really intensified over the summer and autumn. What follows is a summary of some of the published reports to give an idea of what appeared in the press when Britain experienced one of its greatest UFO 'flaps' of all time.

Chart of types of craft observed during international UFO sightings, produced in 1969.

Above: Cromwell Road, Peterborough, as it would have looked when PC Kettle saw the 'mystery airship' above it on 23 March 1909.

Below left: PC James Kettle of the Peterborough Borough Police, the first member of a British uniformed service to spot a 'scareship' in the twentieth century.

Below right: *Punch* magazine's wry comment at the height of the 'scareship' sightings, published on 26 May 1909.

Tyne Dock, South Shields, Tyne and Wear, where Master Stevedore Alexander Mitchell and his working gang had a dramatic sighting of a mystery airship in June 1909.

Zeppelin L3 was one of the two Zeppelins to carry out the first Zeppelin air raid on Britain along the coast of Norfolk on 19 January 1915.

German propaganda card produced to celebrate the first Zeppelin air raid on Britain. Note the artist perpetuates the myth of Zeppelins being fitted with powerful searchlights.

Local people would gather to gaze in wonder at the craters caused by the bombs dropped by Zeppelins on Britain during the First World War.

Members of the Royal Observer Corps watching the skies for enemy aircraft during the Second World War were primed to use the codeword 'Pheno' to report airborne craft that defied identification.

Barrage balloons, key to the anti-aircraft defences of Britain during the Second World War, were also subject to damage by unexplained flying white orbs.

Corporals of an RAF mobile meteorological unit prepare to send up a balloon to measure wind speed and cloud height, January 1940.

Above left: Second World War Chain Home Low radar installation of the type being guarded by Albert Wiltshire at Cresswell Bay in Northumberland when he was abducted by a UFO in 1942.

Above right: *'Griff' on the Gremlin* (1943), one of several booklets containing cartoons of alien-like creatures and the dangerous mischief they got up to on aircraft during the Second World War.

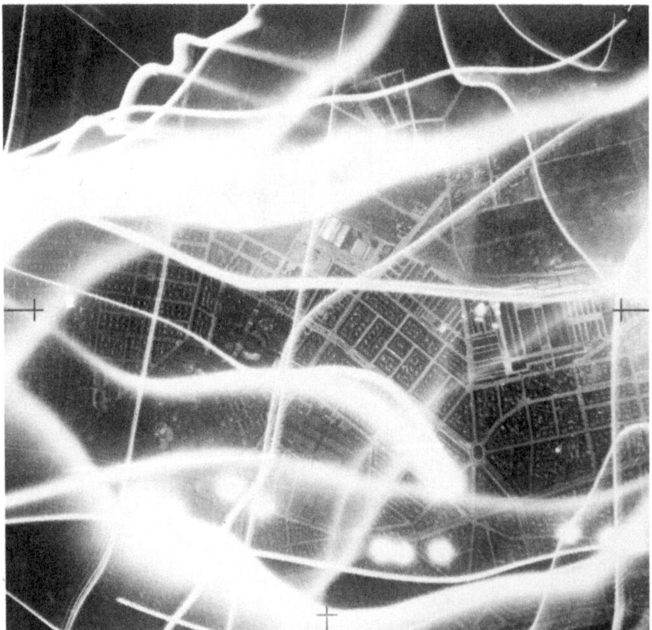

Aerial view from an RAF aircraft over Berlin during an air raid in 1941. The broad, wavy lines are the tracks of German searchlights. Among the many lights seen during aerial attacks, some of them stood out as unexplained.

Right: Lord Hugh Dowding (1882–1970), Air Chief Marshal of RAF Fighter Command during the Battle of Britain in 1940, went on record stating he believed that UFOs exist.

Below: American columnist and investigative reporter Dorothy Kilgallen who reported a remarkable story in 1955 of a UFO brought down during the Second World War and still in Allied hands.

Bottom: Sir Winston Churchill (centre), photographed during a visit to anti-aircraft batteries watching for rockets in June 1944. Churchill maintained a belief and keen interest in UFOs from the 'scareships' of 1909 to the Mainbrace incident of 1952.

WAAF radar operator Denise Miley plotting aircraft on a cathode ray tube in the Receiver Room at Bawdsey Chain Home station, May 1945.

A Royal Air Force Gloster Meteor jet fighter of the type involved in the UFO encounter during Operation Mainbrace, 1952.

Right: Mrs Jessie Roestenburg and her sons Anthony (eight) and Ronald (six) witnessed a huge UFO above the roof of the farmhouse where they lived at Ranton, Staffordshire, on 21 October 1954.

Below: Sky trail and UFO under intelligent control above Pallion, Sunderland, in the 1960s.

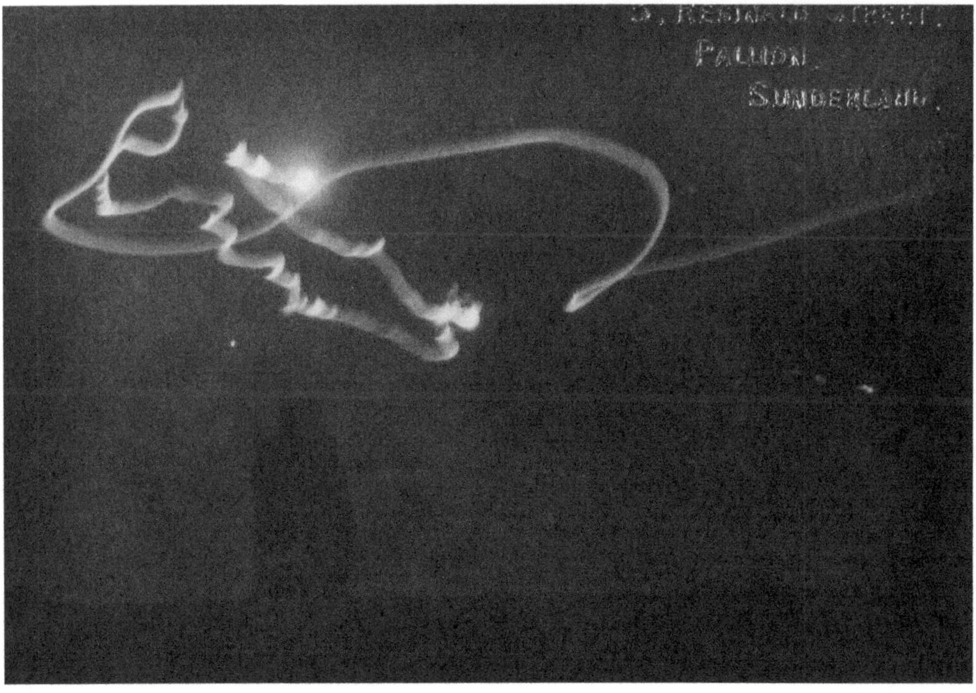

The Penshaw Monument was built in the 1840s in the style of a Greek temple on the top of Penshaw Hill, Sunderland. Many UFOs have been seen here. Could there be a portal in the sky above?

Stonehenge, Salisbury Plain, Wiltshire, is one of the world's most famous prehistoric monuments and a place where UFOs have been regularly sighted.

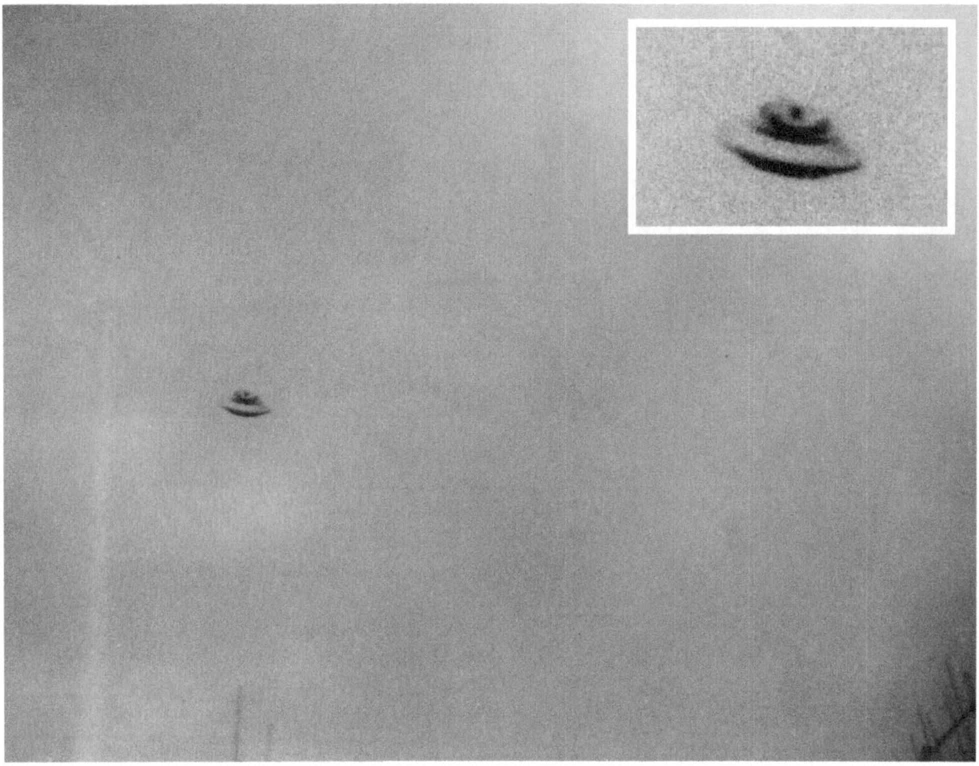

Photo of a UFO over Warminster taken by Gordon Faulkner (twenty-three) from the front doorstep of his home with his Halina 35mm camera at 8.20 p.m. on Sunday 29 August 1965.

Photo of three UFOs taken by Stephen Pratt (fifteen) with his Kodak Instamatic 50 camera from outside his home on Leslie Avenue, Conisborough, Doncaster, South Yorkshire, on Monday 28 March 1966.

Above: Artist's impression of the glowing cross pursued by PCs Roger Willey and Clifford Waycott in a patrol car over the Devon countryside during the early hours of 24 October 1967.

Left: Experts examine one of the six hoax flying saucers that mysteriously appeared at various locations across southern England on 4 September 1967.

Back Lane, Metton, Norfolk. April Fabb set off to cycle over to her married sister on 8 April 1969 and was never seen again. Her bicycle was found in the field beyond the tree on the right.

The Earsdon to Holywell Road, Northumberland, where Lillian Middleton had a terrifying encounter with a UFO on the night of 21 August 1980.

Security fencing at the site of the former east/back gate of RAF Woodbridge from where the mysterious lights in Rendlesham Forest were first spotted on 26 December 1980.

Road from the east gate of RAF Woodbridge leading to Rendlesham Forest, taken by Staff-Sergeant Jim Penniston, A1C John Burroughs and A1C Ed Cabansag to investigate the unexplained lights seen among the trees on 26 December 1980.

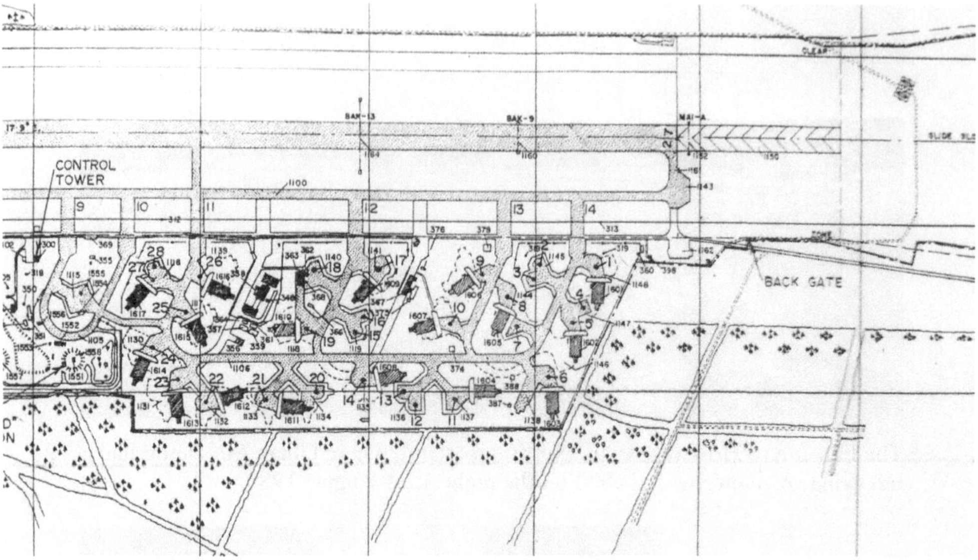

Military map of RAF Woodbridge showing the location of the control tower, runway (top), east/back gate and the road off-site into Rendlesham Forest.

Reconstruction the UFO seen in Rendlesham Forest based on the sketch by Staff-Sergeant Jim Penniston of 26 December 1980.

Right: Colonel Charles I. Halt USAF. At the time of the Rendlesham incident he was Lieutenant Colonel, Deputy Base Commander, witness to the unexplained lights and author of the 'Halt Memorandum'.

Below: The 'Halt Memorandum' on 'Unexplained Lights' in Redlesham Forest by Lieutenant Colonel Charles I. Halt, Deputy Base Commander, dated 31 January 1981.

DEPARTMENT OF THE AIR FORCE
HEADQUARTERS 81ST COMBAT SUPPORT GROUP (USAFE)
APO NEW YORK 09755

REPLY TO ATTN OF: CD — 13 Jan 81

SUBJECT: Unexplained Lights

TO: RAF/CC

1. Early in the morning of 27 Dec 80 (approximately 0300L), two USAF security police patrolmen saw unusual lights outside the back gate at RAF Woodbridge. Thinking an aircraft might have crashed or been forced down, they called for permission to go outside the gate to investigate. The on-duty flight chief responded and allowed three patrolmen to proceed on foot. The individuals reported seeing a strange glowing object in the forest. The object was described as being metalic in appearance and triangular in shape, approximately two to three meters across the base and approximately two meters high. It illuminated the entire forest with a white light. The object itself had a pulsing red light on top and a bank(s) of blue lights underneath. The object was hovering or on legs. As the patrolmen approached the object, it maneuvered through the trees and disappeared. At this time the animals on a nearby farm went into a frenzy. The object was briefly sighted approximately an hour later near the back gate.

2. The next day, three depressions 1 1/2" deep and 7" in diameter were found where the object had been sighted on the ground. The following night (29 Dec 80) the area was checked for radiation. Beta/gamma readings of 0.1 milliroentgens were recorded with peak readings in the three depressions and near the center of the triangle formed by the depressions. A nearby tree had moderate (.05-.07) readings on the side of the tree toward the depressions.

3. Later in the night a red sun-like light was seen through the trees. It moved about and pulsed. At one point it appeared to throw off glowing particles and then broke into five separate white objects and then disappeared. Immediately thereafter, three star-like objects were noticed in the sky, two objects to the north and one to the south, all of which were about 10° off the horizon. The objects moved rapidly in sharp angular movements and displayed red, green and blue lights. The objects to the north appeared to be elliptical through an 8-12 power lens. They then turned to full circles. The objects to the north remained in the sky for an hour or more. The object to the south was visible for two or three hours and beamed down a stream of light from time to time. Numerous individuals, including the undersigned, witnessed the activities in paragraphs 2 and 3.

CHARLES I. HALT, Lt Col, USAF
Deputy Base Commander

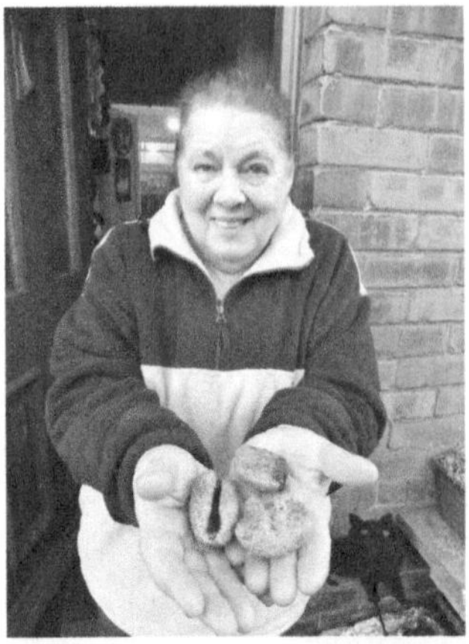

Left: UFO researcher Brenda Butler, co-author of *Sky Crash*, the first book published on the Rendlesham incident, holding some of the strange material recovered from site.

Below: : One of the 1980s radar screens at the RAF Air Defence Radar Museum at Neatishead showing Britain and the French, Belgian and Dutch coasts.

Bottom: The plateau of the Burway at Devil's Mouth among the hills of the Long Mynd near Church Stretton, Shropshire, the scene of recorded UFO activity for decades.

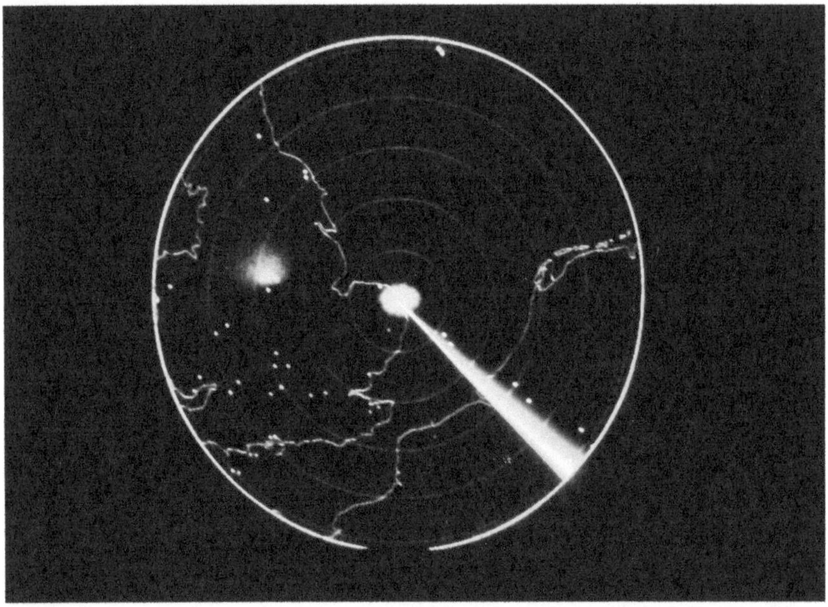

8 June

A large round, rotating and shimmering silver object was seen hovering over marshes at West Caister in Norfolk.

29 June

An 'octopus shaped' object 'as bright as a star' was spotted manoeuvring below wispy cloud in the sky near the ancient and beautiful Wittenham Clumps, Berkshire. The RAF offered an explanation of the 'octopus' actually being the reflection of a searchlight on the base of a cloud.

2 July

Mysterious lights were seen by *News* and *Mail* senior reporter Tony Miller in the sky above Bagshot Hill near Send. An object resembling 'a shimmering football' was also seen hovering over a field and then rising up and down 'in uncanny manner' near the popular beauty spot of Newlands Corner, near Guildford, by Squadron Leader D. Shipwright of Triggs Lane, Woking.

3 July

Four teachers and some 200 boys watched a mysterious orb hovering over the Bearwood near Birmingham. The Edgbaston Observatory and Meteorological Office at Birmingham Airport both agreed it was unlikely to have been a weather balloon.

4 July

An egg- or rugby-ball-shaped object that emitted reddish and sometimes violet light was spotted at 1,000 feet over the coastal town of Cromer, Norfolk. The UFO hovered silently and remained stationary for around two minutes before it departed at incredible speed. Before it moved witnesses noted the side lights of the craft disappeared but the lights at the front remained on.

4 July

A green, glowing object with a bright white centre appeared to land in the Melbourne area of the East Riding of Yorkshire. A similar object was spotted flying over Scarborough at high speed the following day.

6 July

A large object was spotted over Warminster that was apparently under intelligent control, as it was doing complicated manoeuvres in the sky that were impossible for any known aircraft.

8 July

A mysterious object shaped like a humming top with an elliptical top, pointed base and surrounded by a very bright light was observed spinning in the sky above Ollerton, Nottinghamshire.

9 July

A grey-coloured disc surrounded by a silvery glow was spotted through binoculars over Dungeness, Kent.

11 July

A brilliantly lit UFO shaped like a huge piece of classroom chalk with clean-cut edges and a tapered end leading the direction of motion was seen moving rapidly westwards near Shipston-on-Stour, Warwickshire.

11 July

A glowing quarter-moon-shaped object was spotted manoeuvring over the village of Lytchett Maltravers, Dorset.

13 July

A red saucer-shaped object surrounded by a bright halo of light hovered over West Howe, Dorset, then moved slowly away. On the same evening a mysterious purple object flew silently over Wimborne in the same county.

24 July

A 30-foot silver sphere was observed swooping down to earth at an estimated 100 mph then disappeared near Awalton, near Peterborough.

2 August

A flying saucer was spotted moving slowly and silently over Maidstone, Kent, in the early hours of the morning. It disappeared suddenly leaving three or four shafts of light behind it that also soon vanished.

A silent, red, glowing oval-shaped object of some 20 to 30 feet across with a light-coloured hull was reported to have been seen moving slowly over Arbroath, Scotland. It was noted that the electricity supply cut out in the town as the UFO passed over it.

4 August

A bright white light emitting a humming sound shot across the sky over Heysham, Lancashire, in two or three seconds.

5 August

An orange disc that swayed from side to side in the sky and alternately dimmed then brightened sweeping searchlight-like beams passed over Burghfield, Reading.

6 August

A pair of round, silver UFOs were sighted in the sky near Medway Bridge, Kent.

10 August

Two Lancashire County policemen stationed at Hindley, near Wigan, spotted a glowing white orb of over 100 feet in diameter flying east at a fast speed. On the same evening a pair of policemen stationed at Bledbury, near Stockport, spotted a very similar object three hours later.

A pink, glowing and rotating flying saucer, estimated to have been some 80 to 100 feet in diameter, was seen over Farnworth, near Bolton.

A rugby-ball-shaped UFO with blue flashing lights around its edge was spotted over Stafford. The object appeared to be rotating and a sound was emitted in time with each rotation. A red UFO was also seen roaming (and making a strange noise as it did so) over Weston, Staffordshire, for around twenty minutes on the same day.

11 August

A bright orange, spherical UFO was seen near Blackheath, Wolverhampton. The object appeared to split into two halves, both of which gradually got smaller until they disappeared.

15 August

A spherical orange-red object was spotted zig-zagging across the sky near Wigan.

17 August

A triangular-shaped, glowing UFO was seen moving horizontally and disappearing into clouds over Weaverham and Northwich. When observed through binoculars, the object seemed to be spinning and surrounded by lights that changed colour while the centre maintained a steady yellow glow.

A spherical, metallic-looking UFO that 'shone like a mirror' was seen hovering then crossing the sky near Harrogate.

A brilliant white light, seemingly accompanied by a strange humming noise, was observed over Hessle, near Hull.

19 August
A UFO estimated to be 200–300 feet across with windows and purple-green lights passed over Hindley, Wigan. Its approach was preceded by a loud buzzing noise that interfered with television sets and dogs were caused to bark and run around in an alarmed state as it passed overhead.

20 August
A glowing, silver flying saucer with a dome top was spotted in the night sky over Leeds.

22 August
A huge shimmering red disc surrounded by fourteen lights was seen flying fast across the night sky, emitting a hum as it did so, over Burghfield, near Reading.

24 August (approximately)
A bright-orange UFO about the size of a car described as being 'like a pyramid with about three quarters of the top chopped off and one corner longer than the others' was seen hovering over trees at St Germans, Cornwall. It was seen turning upside down, then circled around and disappeared.

24 August
A large illuminated flying saucer surrounded by a circle of orange light was reported as hovering over North Shields, Northumberland.

25 August (approximately)
At least a dozen orange orbs appeared in the sky over Ramsbottom, Manchester. Witnesses stated the orbs grew bigger, stopped, then faded out. At one point they shone out a beam of light below them.

28 August
Two bright elliptical, orange lights surrounded by a luminous halo were seen hovering silently in the sky over Stoke-on-Trent.

29 August
A mysterious glowing object was seen racing across the sky over Congresbury, Somerset.

A dome-shaped UFO showing alternating red and orange lights was seen flying slowly and silently towards Talke, Staffordshire. It disappeared then reappeared an hour later.

30 August (approximately)
A tremendously bright and shiny UFO shaped like a spinning top was spotted climbing high in the sky and emitting a hum over Old Trafford, Manchester.

30 August
Hindley, Wigan, was visited by another UFO. This time it was a conical, silver object with green and purple lights down its side and an orange dome on top. The object was observed to hover and zig-zag across the sky.

A large, red, glowing orb surrounded by a ring of glowing lights was spotted travelling slow and low in the sky over Northwich.

The Clifton Saucer

A number of the national papers of 6 July 1967 carried the story that more than 100 people claimed they saw a flying saucer land. The bulk of the witnesses were on high ground near Fairham Comprehensive School at Clifton, Nottingham. This news spread fast and it was reported 'housewives rushed from their homes' when they heard that 'a disc-shaped silvery saucer' about 30 feet long had come down. Concerned residents reported the matter to the police and they searched the area but found no trace of anything having landed. A police spokesman was quick to dismiss what people had seen as 'an optical illusion caused by sunlight and a cloud of dust'. But witnesses like Mrs Marjorie Cowdell of High Bank, Clifton, were adamant: 'I don't care what the police say, I saw a flying saucer swoop to the ground.' Neither the Air Ministry nor Met Office could offer possible causes of what had been seen.

On the same day more than 200 miles away Mr Ron Woods of Farnborough was camping in the New Forest, Hampshire, when he spotted a huge ball of white light careering through the sky. It crashed between Brockenhurst and Highcliffe with a terrific explosion and animals stampeded he said. Dozens of holidaymakers were also alarmed. Coastguards at Southbourne, Hampshire, said they presumed it was a meteorite. Police searched the area but found nothing.

Domed Craft Over the Derwent Valley

On 18 July 1967 Brian Ford (twenty-three), a machine operator of No. 16 West Lane, Allendale Cottages, was out walking in his local countryside at dusk and had been watching young foxes playing in a wooded copse when he happened to look up. They appeared as dome-shaped, dark objects in the sky, quite low and directly over the valley. 'As darkness closed in, they just lit up.' Mr Ford rushed home to tell his wife Eunice, who initially laughed it off but when she looked out across the Derwent Valley towards Hedley, sure enough there were six dome-shaped objects on the horizon. She also could not really believe what she was seeing, so she alerted her neighbours. Mrs Linda Reay (twenty-five) told a reporter: 'I saw six lights (oval shaped and orange in colour) in formation at about 2.00am. I watched them for about half an hour. They were moving about and then they hovered before moving away out of sight...I was so disturbed I did not sleep all night.'

The Bentilee UFO Landing

Just after 9 p.m. on the evening of Saturday 2 September 1967 children playing outside a house in Beverly Drive on the Bentilee housing estate, Stoke-on-Trent, spotted a glowing flying saucer over the rooftops. One of the children shouted, 'There's a flying saucer!'

Mrs Stephenson came out of her house, spotted it too, and called to her neighbour, Mrs Bowen, 'Look at that thing in the sky.'

Mrs Bowen described what she saw: 'It seemed like a saucer... It changed in different colours - a red, a greenish and a blue ... It was like a wind when it came over but there was no sound.' It then appeared to land in a field beyond the end of the adjacent Wendline Close. Mrs Stephenson described what she saw after the landing: 'The object glowed bright red as if someone had lit a bonfire in the middle of a field. It spanned half a field. We could see the outline of it clearly like a dome but we couldn't see no door. There was no heat it was just a red glow ... We couldn't even hear a bird, everything was dead.'

They were joined on the street by another neighbour who had been in his bedroom, which had been illuminated by the red glow. He thought the field was on fire and had come down to see what was going on. Meanwhile, the children had run off towards where the saucer had landed. Mrs Bowen and Mrs Stephenson followed behind and saw it in the field: a domed saucer that was glowing bright red. A police sergeant and two constables who happened to be passing in their van were also soon on the scene. The children and adults informed them of what they had seen, and they started to climb the banks. Mindful of the young ages of some of the children, one of the police constables sent the younger children back home. As the policemen were climbing the bank the UFO suddenly sped skywards, reaching about 300 feet in the air. It then hovered for ten or twelve seconds, then zoomed off in the direction it had come. By the time the policemen reached the top of the bank, at least according to the constable interviewed on the TV news, there was nothing to be seen apart from the glow from the windows of a nearby pub.

The Bentilee incident was thoroughly investigated by amateur astronomers Roger Stanway and Tony Pace, who managed to interview one of the police officers who had attended. He admitted they had seen a light in the sky but claimed it had gone out almost as soon as they turned to look at it. They ventured the suggestion it might have been a car headlight. Stanway and Pace published their findings, along with details of seventy other sightings in the Staffordshire area, in their excellent booklet *Flying Saucer Report* (1968). After having interviewed numerous independent witnesses, many of whom had been worried and disturbed by what they had seen, Stanway and Pace approached the MoD in London and submitted their initial report seeking answers. In an interview on ATV News in November 1969 Stanway explained they were granted a meeting about the incident. They asked the MoD officer if the incident described in their report actually did take place. The reply was 'Yes', but when pressed to see if the MoD could offer any explanation for it his reply was simple: 'We have no idea.'

The Great British UFO Hoax

With so much about flying saucers appearing in the press, it was not unusual when six mysterious 'flying saucers' appeared as if they had landed at various locations across southern England on 4 September 1967. The 'saucers' were found at Queenborough on the Isle of Sheppey; Sundridge Park golf course in Bromley, South London; Winkfield, near Ascot; Welford in Berkshire; Chippenham in Wiltshire; and on Dial Hill in Clevedon, Somerset. These mysterious objects caused a major incident response involving several police forces, troops from Southern Command, army bomb-disposal units and even an RAF helicopter was used for the removal of the 'saucer' found on the Isle of Sheppey.

Each 'saucer' measured 54 inches long, 30 inches wide and 20 inches deep, weighed 100 pounds and emitted an odd electronic sound when it was flipped over. Once one of the 'saucers' was opened it was found to contain a foul-smelling goo that turned out to be a mixture of flour and water that had fermented inside the casing. The casing itself was discovered to have been made of two halves of moulded fibreglass coated in metal, and the strange sound they emitted was generated by electronic gadgets inside.

The whole thing turned out to be a hoax perpetrated by Farnborough Royal Aircraft Establishment apprentices and sci-fi fans Christopher Southall (twenty-one) and Roger Palmer (twenty-one) to raise funds during Rag Week. Teams of helpers placed the 'saucers' under the cover of darkness in areas where they would be found by passing members of the public. The pranksters revealed the hoax the day the 'saucers' were found; the news story appeared on national tv and in newspapers around the world and they raised £2,000 for charity. Fortunately for Christopher and Roger, no legal action was taken against them. One Bromley police officer summed it up by saying: 'We are taking it like gentlemen.'

The Byker Saucer

On the clear night of 3 October 1967, Newcastle policeman PC Dawson (twenty-five) was patrolling Shields Road, Byker, when at 1.25 a.m. he saw a silver-grey circular object in the sky around the same size as a full moon but three times as bright. He also heard an intermittent regular-pitch noise 'like a car with a loose fan belt ... it was quite high ... it then moved away west towards Tyne Bridge and the sound faded. I have no idea what it could have been. It was very strange.' Not without some personal trepidation, he rang his station sergeant at Headlam Street police station to report he had just seen and heard a flying saucer. He need not have worried, as other policemen at the station had also heard the noise, which lasted for more than a minute.

Several people in Byker had also seen the object. Among them was Sharkey's taxi driver Gordon Armstrong of Hotspur Street, Heaton who was in the taxi office when he heard it. He recalled how: 'The air was vibrating and I looked out and saw a strange grey object. There was a flash. It sounded like something hovering then accelerated away.' Mr Edward Jobe, manager of the taxi office, added: The noise was like an unoiled spring unwinding. Several people came out to watch and cars stopped in the street. The air was almost electric.'

The Tyne Dock Triangles

On the evening of 21 October 1967 residents in a block of flats at Tyne Dock, South Shields, had a grandstand view to see a formation of three glowing UFOs hovering in the sky over their homes on Dock Street.

Some could hardly believe their eyes and stood outside to watch the sight; they were also joined by a policeman who was out on patrol. One resident, Mrs Marguerite Smith, her son John and another relation all watched the flying saucers for thirty minutes until they finally moved off and disappeared over Newcastle.

Mrs Smith described what she saw as: 'Triangular in shape and glowed so brightly that they dazzled my eyes. I have seen nothing like them before.' The policeman was dumbfounded and just stood and stared. Mrs Smith's husband, Ron, a miner, also saw the objects: 'They seemed to move one above the other and glowed very brightly.' A police spokesman commented: 'The people reported to us that they had seen the objects but we are not making any inquiries.'

Police in High-speed Pursuit of UFO

Police Constables Roger Willey and Clifford Waycott experienced one of the most infamous sightings in British UFO history during the early hours of 24 October 1967. Willey and Waycott, who were based at Okehampton, Devon, were out on night duty in patrol car Delta 9 with PC Willey driving from Holsworthy to Hatherleigh along the A3072 when they spotted a bright, radiating, cross-shaped 'brilliant white, brilliant light ... brighter than anything else in the sky other than the moon ... with inner parts somewhat similar to the points of a compass and they were somewhat blurred'. The cross-shaped light first appeared ahead of the policemen on the right side of the road at Anvil Corner. Both agreed that it seemed to be 400 yards away from them, at treetop level, and seemed to be keeping up with their police car. They wound down the window to get a better look but still could not identify what it was, so they radioed in and began to chase the light. PC Waycott maintained a commentary of the chase as it took place over the next 14 miles.

Travelling at speeds in excess of 80 mph, the mysterious light always kept ahead of them at the same distance. Both officers agreed the acceleration of the cross-shaped light from the patrol car 'was terrific'. By now, the light was to the north of the road and seemed to accelerate away from them over Black Torrington. The two policemen stopped at the garage east of Narracott Cross. They thought a static light nearby may have been the UFO, but upon investigation that light turned out to be on a farmhouse.

The police officers returned to their car and drove towards Hatherleigh and Okehampton, but it was not long before they saw the cross-shaped light again. It was never in sight for long as it was often obscured by trees they passed along the road. Around a mile south of Hatherleigh, the two constables stopped their car near a parked vehicle and awoke Christopher Garner who was asleep inside; he too saw the star-shaped light as it travelled into the east.

The light had been under observation and pursuit by the police officers from 4.01 a.m. until 5 a.m. The story made the national press and was even covered by television news programmes that featured interviews with both officers. When asked if they were close enough to the object to be absolutely certain their eyes were not fooling them, both officers were certain they had not been mistaken. Exeter Police headquarters telephoned the Meteorological Office, RAF Chivenor and Exeter Airport but were informed by all of them that there was nothing in the sky that night that could account for the sighting. PCs Waycott and Willey were convinced that the object had been under intelligent control; indeed, both officers were convinced the object had been observing them.

The following night police officers in five police cars across East Sussex saw what they described as a 'bright flying cross' in the early hours of the morning. Reports of a similar light were made in Wales.

Night of the UFOs

On one night alone, 26/27 October 1967, numerous reports were received from across the country – from the north of England to the south coast. One of the first sightings on 26 October was by the driver of a Brighton bus travelling on the coastal road at Saltdean, east of Brighton, who saw what he described as a cigar-shaped object surrounded by a bright green glow emitting sparks from its tail, which travelled parallel with the bus for a short time.

Shortly before midnight on 26 October, Allen Armstrong of Foxhills Crescent, Lanchester, spotted a huge ice-blue star travelling at tremendous speed over County Durham as he was driving home from Stanley. He recalled: 'I was quite startled. It appeared to be a bright bluish light pointed at the forward end and flared behind. It came from behind me and travelled through about 40 degrees in three seconds, then went out of sight behind a row of houses.' At 2.45 a.m. farmer Richard Robinson of South Ouston Farm at Stamfordham awoke and spotted a weird object in the sky from the bedroom window. He woke his wife and they watched it together, describing it as 'like a starfish with an elongated tail'. The object was travelling south along the course of the Tyne. The white light was diffused and the object was very much brighter than the stars. It was the size of a shilling at arm's length and moving very slowly. It was observed for 30 minutes. Enquiries were made with RAF Ouston and an official stated there were no aircraft in the area at the time.

At 4.40 a.m. Mrs Monica McLaughlin and her daughter of Cramwell Court, Stella Park, Blaydon-on-Tyne, were awakened by what Mrs McLaughlin thought was someone revving a high-powered motor. Looking out of her bedroom window, she saw a strange electric-blue cone-shaped object with an orange periphery in the sky. The whole effect was dazzling. After hovering over Dunston power station for a few minutes it developed a haze and changed shape to oval, then vanished. Five minutes later it reappeared: again, hovering over the power station and emitting a brilliant blue glow. Mother and daughter observed the object for a further seven minutes then went back to bed.

Another UFO was spotted over Wallsend, North Tyneside, by Mrs Jean Craig and her friend while on their way to work at 5.48 a.m. They saw 'a round tea plate sized object with two spikes on ... it was huge in the sky. It was like a silver flying cross and it was revolving in an anti-clockwise motion.' It was observed by the ladies for about ten minutes.

Police Constable Earnshaw was on duty at Bacup police station, Lancashire, on 27 October 1967 when he picked up severe interference on the station's radio receiver. Going outside to investigate, he saw a cigar-shaped object about 50 feet in length by 10 feet in diameter hovering an estimated 250 feet above the police station. He watched the objects for a couple of minutes and could discern a light-coloured metallic UFO that gave off an incandescent glow, and a low whirring noise could be heard. What appeared to be portholes ran along the length of the object, but there was no visible signs of propulsion. PC Earnshaw was soon joined by two more officers who watched the UFO with him until it flew off in the direction of Bacup golf course. Two constables followed the object in a police car along a hillside behind the police station, but the object rose vertically and made off at a fantastic speed in the Burnley direction then disappeared.

Meanwhile, a bright cross-shaped object which moved from side to side and at one time hovered over Glossop, Derbyshire, was spotted by police officers. Six men from the nearby Cheshire Constabulary and two members of the public made separate sightings of the object, which remained in view for three-quarters of an hour.

A spokesman at the Royal Observatory commented that they had received two reports of the Glossop sighting and one from Manchester, only 13 miles from the town. The time of the sighting, early morning, immediately roused astronomers' suspicions and suggested what witnesses had actually seen could have been Jupiter or the brightness of Venus coming through low cloud.

The Ibsley Sighting

Long-distance lorry driver Carl Farlow was travelling along the main Salisbury–Bournemouth road at Ibsley late on the night of 5 November 1967. It was about 11.30 p.m. and a 12-foot-long cigar-shaped object with a white dome underneath landed in the road in front of his truck. His headlights immediately went out, as did those of a Jaguar car that was travelling in the opposite direction and both vehicles stopped. The landed UFO sat on the road enigmatically showing green lights. After around two minutes the UFO took off and sped off to the east and the lights on the lorry and the Jaguar came on again.

Cigar-shaped Object Over Walton

On 7 November 1967 Fred Bissell was asleep in his bed at his home at Walton near Clacton-on-Sea, Essex, when a bright light shining through his window woke him up at 4.30 a.m. Looking out, he saw what he described as an object hovering silently over Walton Pier. As it hovered the UFO moved backwards and forwards with a bright light beaming down from it. Suddenly, the UFO sped off at a terrific speed towards Harwich, turning on its side as it did so to resemble a cigar. It then returned to hover over the pier before shooting off to the south. Two police officers at nearby Clacton reported seeing orange lights in the sky at the same time.

UFO Terrorises Teacher in Shropshire

Science teacher Jerry Richmond had been to a dance with his girlfriend. He had taken her home to Bridgnorth and was driving back to his home in Sparkhill, Birmingham, along the Bridgnorth–Wolverhampton road at the village of Hilton at 1.30 a.m. on 26 July 1968 when he first saw the UFO:

> I was doing about 40mph when I saw it rise from behind a clump of trees by a low fence on the left of the road. At this time it was elliptical in shape, and the closest I was to it. It was only 30-40 yards away. I estimate it to have been about 90-100ft long. It had a flat, dull, steady glow. It rose to about 500ft and then descended at the same speed. I first thought it was a weather balloon but I immediately dismissed

> that possibility because of the speed it moved, its size and the apparent lack of wind.
>
> After rising and falling at a steady speed, the object shot across the road then started to zig-zag towards me … I placed my hand on the outside of the windscreen and I drove along to make sure the object wasn't a reflection. It wasn't. As it zig-zagged towards me, I estimated it to be about 30ft wide. By this time I was really worried. I just had no idea what the thing was.

Feeling panic setting in, Jerry accelerated away but the UFO followed him for about five miles until it disappeared over a hill. A car approached and Jerry flashed his lights to try and get the driver to stop, but he passed by. Then the UFO reappeared:

> It appeared again on the left and came towards and over the top of my car and turned and went ahead of me. It looked as though it had a tail of some kind, something like a helicopter viewed from underneath. After repeated zig-zags, the object hovered over a clump of trees on the right-hand side of the road. [By that time] it was a definite cigar shape and only about 100 yards away. I was panic-stricken. There seemed to be a light from the object shining on the top of the trees as it hovered there. Then it shot off into the distance … That was the last I saw of it, but its speed was fantastic. The whole thing from first to last took about 10-15 minutes.

The Missing Girl

The salutary warning given to the author of this book and many other youngsters growing up in Norfolk in the 1970s and 1980s when we were going out on our bicycles to visit friends was to 'Remember April Fabb'. We were made only too aware the story of the young girl who had gone out on her bicycle one day and 'never came home'.

Originally receiving huge press and television coverage, searches were conducted and there was a massive police investigation in 1969 after April disappeared, but by the time the story was retold to us Norfolk youngsters in the late 1970s the details had become distant. The *Weekend Book of Ghosts and Horror* (1982), edited by Richard Whittington Egan, revisited the story of thirteen-year-old April Fabb in a chapter titled 'April's Last Ride'. It details how April set out from her family home at Metton on the afternoon of 8 April 1969 to visit her older, married sister in Roughton. It should only have been a short ride of little over a mile through rural countryside and fairly straight roads; she could have got there in about ten minutes. She was never seen again.

April had vanished. It was every parent's worst nightmare come true. All that was found was her bicycle, which had been thrown over a verge into a field on the road where she would have been cycling along. Under such circumstances, tragically, it is highly probable that April was abducted by some vile individual. However, the 'weird and unnatural aspects' of the disappearance mentioned in the chapter of *The Weekend Book of Ghosts and Horror* contemplated the distance April's bicycle had been found from the narrow country road where she had been riding it.

No footprints had been seen in the ploughed soil of the field where the bicycle had been found and it would have taken 'superhuman strength' to throw it over the verge and several feet clear into the field, or perhaps it had even 'been lifted up and dropped from a great height' as if perhaps she had been taken skyward in some tractor beam. Some people, as the article suggested, would become firmly of the opinion she had been 'whisked away by an evil power, possibly even from another planet'.

Is this truly as far-fetched as it sounds? There are urban legends around the UK of cyclists being caught in beams from above and levitated off the ground as if by a tractor beam. In fact, there are cases to be found all over the world, including that from Brazil little over a year after April's disappearance on 16 July 1970. Sr Marcelino of Papagaios, Brazil, was cycling home from work on a rough and infrequently used country road when he encountered a 'headlight' shining down from the sky from an unknown source. His ears were filled with a deafening noise and suddenly he and his bicycle were suspended in the air. He desperately tried to jump from his bicycle, but was unable to do so; he simply could not move, and when he tried to call out for help no sound came out. After being suspended in mid-air for what seemed like a few minutes he was set down on the ground again, and he attempted to pedal off at speed. Just as he thought he was making ground he was lifted up again, except this time it was in total silence. Fortunately, he was set down again and cycled home as fast as he could.

Our final thoughts must be with April and her family. A notice was pinned on the door of Metton Church (just across the way from where April lived with her family) for years afterwards that read: 'Will you of your charity remember in your prayers April Fabb, a child who disappeared from this parish in April 1969 of whom nothing has since been heard. Please also remember the parents and relatives who still wait and hope.' These words have now been carved upon a memorial stone to April outside the church. Both her parents have now passed away and they are buried at the foot of the stone. The fate of April Fabb remains undiscovered to this day; her family and friends have never forgotten her.

The Docking Incident

At twenty-five minutes past midnight on Thursday 19 June 1969 radio and television engineer Robin Peck (twenty-eight) of the village of Docking, Norfolk, was driving home from King's Lynn in his Ford Thames van. While travelling along the Bircham to Docking road, about 2 miles from Docking, the headlights of his van went dim and the engine started to misfire badly. He pulled onto the side of the road, then suddenly everything just cut out and would not restart. Releasing the bonnet catch, he got out and went to check the engine.

Setting foot onto the road, he immediately experienced a feeling 'as if the air was full of static electricity' and the hair on his head, arms and legs all felt as if it was standing on end. Only then did he become aware of an object in the sky about a quarter of a mile away and between 100 to 150 feet above the ground. He described it as being around 40 feet wide and having the appearance of a luminous blue inverted mushroom. It was clearly defined but had an aura of golden light around it that stretched down towards ground level. There were no visible markings or features such as windows. There was no smell nor sound.

Robin looked at his watch and saw the luminous 'points' had come 'alive' and the luminosity of the hands increased 100 per cent (curiously, after the incident the watch was no longer luminous). Gazing at his watch for a while, transfixed by its powerful glow and wondering what he should do next, he saw the UFO speed smoothly away at terrific speed in the direction of King's Lynn. Robin then returned to sit in his van and he tried starting the engine. Everything responded normally again and, although shaken by the incident, he managed to drive home.

On that same night, Kenneth Woodhouse of Norwich Road, Costessey, who was employed as a burner at the local engineering company of Boulton & Paul on Riverside, Norwich, was walking parallel with the river when he happened to look up and spotted a mysterious orb that glowed brightly with a bluish tinge which was moving right to left over Norwich Cathedral. Meanwhile, Stanley Watson of Hill Road, New Costessey, was in bed between 12.15 and 12.30 when his wife sat up in bed and exclaimed, 'Good God, what was that?' They saw, through the closed curtains of the window, a ball of brilliant light about the size of a football, almost like a full moon, but travelling far too fast for this.

The Irthlingborough Landing

A number of children in the village of Irthlingborough, Northamptonshire, claimed to have seen a UFO on the evening of 15 July 1969. Young sisters Sharon and Denise Cuddihy said they looked out from their bedroom window and saw a red flashing object land in a field near the village. After it landed the girls said it turned into a number of flashing lights and the sky seemed to turn a pale blue colour at the same time. The girls fetched their father, who came to look but could not explain what he was seeing. Several other children also spotted the UFO, including five young lads out camping for the night. Kevin Spence (eleven) was one of them. He explained how the UFO 'came hurtling through the air and flashing on and off red'. He thought it had landed in the barley field at the back on the house, but cautious mothers did not allow their children to go and investigate.

Terror of the Bolton Triangle

The Bolton *Evening News* of 26 August 1969 carried the story of Mrs Ann Unsworth of Morris Green Lane and her daughter Carol (fourteen). They were looking out of the window of their back bedroom at dusk when they were terrified to see a huge triangular UFO heading towards their home. The triangle was surrounded by flickering green lights with bright oval lights – one red and two green – at the corners. Mrs Unsworth could not offer an exact idea of size, other than it was huge. The UFO was silent and hovered over the chimneys of neighbouring houses for about ten seconds as if it was scanning the area, then it moved off in the direction of a nearby golf course. Both mother and daughter were shaken by what they saw and were so frightened they could not speak for some time afterwards. Mrs Sandra Kirkham, who lived on Normanby Street in the same area, was getting into her car when she spotted the same object. She called to her husband to come and see it, but by the time he arrived on the street it had passed overhead and disappeared.

Firemen Fear Crash Landing of UFO

The *Evening News* of 26 August 1969 ran the story of three Bolton firemen, Sub Officer Eric Dyer, Fireman James Hall and Fireman Bruce Robinson, who were attending a small blaze on Raike Lane when they saw a brilliant white object of 'tremendous size' travelling at a fantastic speed appear as if it was going to crash land on the town but veered off at the last minute and disappeared in the direction of Great Lever. In all they estimated the UFO was in vision for seven seconds. Four other men on the scene also witnessed the UFO pass over.

Triangular UFO Over Yorkshire

Lesley Mason (nineteen) was driving her boyfriend John Steel (twenty) along the Holmpton–Patrington road in the East Riding of Yorkshire late on the night of 10 November 1969 when a mystery triangular object of white light flew across the road in front of the car. Lesley hammered on the brakes only to see to her horror that the UFO wheeled around and was flying in their direction, descending the whole time. As Lesley turned the car around to go and report what had happened to the police at Withernsea, the couple thought the UFO had landed in a nearby field. When the police were told about the incident, they were informed it had already been seen once by a policeman. Chief Inspector W. P. Barraclough told the local press that they were investigating the report of the UFO and they had already established that two aircraft had been in the area at the time of the sighting.

Chapter 5

The 1970s

UFO Auto Stop Near Hinckley

The *Leicester Mercury* of 26 May 1971 reported the experience of Eunice Rose of Hinckley, who had been visiting friends at Oddsone and had left to drive home at 10.50 p.m. Driving alone in her car, she was about to join the main Ashby to Hinckley road at Belchar's Bar when she spotted a glow in the sky towards Ibstock. At first she wondered if it was a ditched car that had ended up with its headlights shining skywards. As she joined the main road and was driving towards Hinckley the glow showed itself to be a UFO 'about the size of a double-decker bus' that passed directly over her car travelling in the direction of Oddstone. As it did so her car engine faded out of power, all the car lights, including the headlights dimmed and the transistor radio that was playing faded out and went dead. Eunice was stricken with fear and she described her hair as 'bristling up'. Once the UFO had passed over the car sprang back to life. Although shaken by her experience, she managed to drive home.

Policemen See UFO Over Nuneaton

The Nuneaton *Evening Tribune* of 24 February 1971 ran the story of four Coventry policemen spotting a UFO over Nuneaton earlier that day. PC Brian Hewitt of Foleshill Police Station was one of them and told his story:

> We were attending a job at Lythalls Lane at 6.15am when we saw a strange thing in the sky. It was not a meteorite or anything like that. There were three single white lights in the sky over Nuneaton area and moving at a great speed in a westerly direction towards Birmingham.

> Then they turned northwards. They were at a height of about two miles and the lights did not belong to the same object because they were so far apart. They appeared to be in formation and were travelling at a tremendous speed … I checked with air traffic control at Birmingham airport and the first aircraft to land there was 45 minutes later than the time we saw the lights.

Flying Saucer Over Tynemouth

At 11.15 p.m. on 15 August 1971, mathematics teacher Wolfgang von Metz spotted a UFO hovering over Tynemouth Castle from his home on Percy Gardens, Tynemouth, Northumberland. Hardly believing what he was seeing he called upon his neighbour, engineer Geoffrey O'Brady-Jones, who he did not know well before that night, to join him at his telescope and confirm what he was seeing.

Both von Metz and O'Brady-Jones described the object as looking 'like a disc seen from the side' with red tips and surrounded by a bluish haze as it hovered. Metz stated: 'the object was solid and under control. It was very clear in the telescope and out drawing coincided exactly. It could not have been the result of heavenly bodies, reflections or anything man-made, unless the RAF was testing a new type of silent flying machine.' As the pair maintained their vigil of the mysterious craft in the sky for the next three hours, they 'saw the object spin, increase in its size and brightness, a red glow appeared on its lower side and bluish haze appeared on the other'. Eventually it just disappeared into the night sky.

The Ripponden Road Enigma

John Taylor (thirty) and his wife Sandra (twenty-nine) were driving back from Newcastle to their Heald Green home at about 2 a.m. on 17 August 1972 and were on the Ripponden Road between York and Thirsk when Sandra told John to pull up. Sandra had spotted something that fitted the description of a flying saucer in a field beside the road. John described it as a melon-shaped structure 'glowing a weird luminous colour' with a tapering base with a 'T' shaped door'. They got out of the car to see if they could get a better look at it, but could not see the base of the thing because of a high hedge. As they watched, the door of the object began to open but they didn't feel like hanging around to see who or what might be opening it, so they rapidly got back into their car and fled. When they arrived back home Mrs Taylor contacted Cheadle Hume police. Part of her expected to be met with scepticism, but she was told other people had reported witnessing the same thing.

The Buttertubs UFO Incident

In the early morning of Saturday 24 March 1973 Alan Blades (seventeen) of Hawes had dropped his girlfriend off and was driving the 6 miles home over the bleak Buttertubs Pass that connected Wensleydale with Swaledale in the Yorkshire Dales. As he approached his downhill home run to Hawes he spotted a red, glowing, oval UFO above his car between the vehicle and Stags Fell. Alan told a *Northern Echo* reporter: 'At first I thought the car lights were shining on something, but when I stopped and switched them off it was still there. I did not dare switch the engine off in case it would not start again. At first it was upright but then seemed to cant to one side and move slowly away. As I watched it seemed that the underpart was spinning. By this time I was scared stiff and set off for home. As I approached the first house at Simonside it had been keeping pace with me, but then suddenly it accelerated to the South East.' The UFO then departed and Alan made it home.

The Berwyn Mountains Incident

On the evening of 23 January 1974, farmer Hugh Edwards saw a mysterious glowing object 'about the size of a bus' in the sky over the Berwyn Mountains in the Llandrillo area of Merionethshire, Wales. As he watched he saw the object dip towards earth and disappear into a valley.

Local residents then heard a 'phenomenally big explosion'. Some of them were interviewed by the BBC after the incident and they spoke of how they had heard bombs exploding during the Second World War and were convinced it was 'far bigger than anything like that'. The explosion was then followed by earth tremors for several minutes afterwards; indeed, the Institute of Geological Sciences (now the British Geological Survey) registered a magnitude 3.5 earthquake in the area at 8.38 p.m. which had been felt as far as 50 miles away.

Locals ran onto the streets in fear and concern. Some of them claimed to have seen a glowing object and lights on the remote mountainside of Cadair Berwyn where there was not normally any lights at all. Many thought some terrible disaster had occurred, such as a plane crash. Emergency services were alerted and search and rescue parties were hastily raised and headed towards the glow on the mountainside, but when they approached up the narrow mountain roads they found police and armed military personnel were already in the area. The volunteer rescue parties were told to stand down and were sent back.

District Nurse Pat Evans was one of those who thought there had been a plane crash and drove up in the family car with her daughters Diane and Tina to see if she could help offer first aid. They drove a good distance along the narrow mountain road and Pat said that to their left they could see a 'huge ball' that was glowing orange-red sitting on the mountain. Her daughters recall how Pat stopped the car and the three of them started looking for what they thought was going to be a crashed aircraft on fire. They were fearful there might be bodies among the wreckage but they were stunned when all they saw was the glowing ball; there were no flames, just the uniform, spherical shape of it and the pulsating orange-red light.

Pat and her daughters were still some distance from the object and they were was not close enough to see exactly what was going on in the darkness, but from their location the object did not appear damaged in any way. They could see lights zig-zagging towards the glowing object, which they thought were probably from a rescue party approaching the site, but on reflection they did wonder how a search party from the village could have got there quite so quickly. Ruth encountered military and police search parties soon afterwards and she was told she needed to leave the area.

Roadblocks were soon set up and areas of the mountainside were sealed off for several days afterwards. The police search of the area was called off later that night and a search and rescue team from RAF Valley on Anglesey were scrambled the following morning to search for any signs of a crashed aircraft. The official line to the media was that nothing was found.

The incident received both the local and national media attention. Recently declassified Ministry of Defence documents suggest the incident at Berwyn had been caused by the combined effects of an earthquake and a meteor crashing onto the mountainside, but considering the sound of the explosion and the lack of a crater caused by meteorite or any other object, some locals and researchers beg to differ. It is no wonder this incident has been referred to as 'the Welsh Roswell'.

The Aveley Abduction

John and Sue Day set off to travel the twenty minutes back home to Aveley, Essex, with their three children, Karen (eleven), Kevin (ten) and Stuart (seven), in their Vauxhall Victor estate at 9.50 p.m. after a visit to Sue's parents on 27 October 1974. Heading south, about a mile out of Hornchurch Kevin spotted a light above terraced houses on their left. Pointing it out to his parents, they saw something like a big star that was oval in shape and emitting a bluish iridescent light. It seemed to be travelling along with their car, then suddenly it changed direction, gathered speed and flashed over them.

As they came onto Aveley Road John and Sue began to feel a sense of panic as they realised the car was still moving but there was no longer any sound from the engine. As the car came out of a bend they hit a bank of quite dense fog with a strange green hue to it. At this point the car radio began to crackle loudly and appeared to have burnt out as a wisp of smoke issued from it. John reached to the radio's wires behind the dash and yanked them out, and as he did so the internal car lights cut out and the vehicle began to lurch along the road. The car suddenly became very cold and John and Sue had the surreal experience of no longer feeling that they were in motion at that moment.

They travelled through the fog for half a mile before they cleared it. Oddly, John felt alone in the car for the next half mile until Sue sat up with a start, asking: 'Is everybody here?' John drove on and, as he did so, warmth and internal lights were restored. The couple spoke about their odd experience in the mist until they reached home. When they pulled in they checked the time, fully expecting it to be about 10.20 p.m., but it turned out it was 1 a.m. in the morning. At no point had they knowingly stopped the car, got caught in a tailback or taken a wrong turning.

Where that lost time had gone deeply troubled the couple. Snatches of memories began to occur and eventually John had three sessions of hypnotic regression. Between John and Sue, a story could be pieced together of how after they entered that strange mist they had suddenly found themselves on a spacecraft where both were subjected to examinations, interacted with the aliens on board and were shown around the craft.

UFO Terrifies Bolton Receptionist

Receptionist Shelley Barnes (seventeen) was returning home from work at 6.05 p.m. on 23 January 1976 when she spotted a brilliant light over an area of land where houses were being built near Rumworth Lodge Reservoir, Bolton, Lancashire. She described it as looking like a car headlight in the sky, but suddenly, and without any warning, the light shot towards her at an incredible speed – she thought it must have been at a mile a second. It then stopped and hovered over the rooftops in front of her. Shelley could see that the object had a width of 20–25 feet, was metallic, had 'flat topped diagonal' form and was rounded underneath.

She could also see the UFO had two lights, one red and one amber, which seemed to glow from within. The rim of the object was surrounded by a 'diffuse whitish glow' that disappeared as the UFO appeared to tilt away from her and it began to spin extremely fast. As it began to spin Shelley experienced 'a peculiar grinding sensation in her lower teeth'. Shelly was terrified and ran off, leaving the object hovering above the rooftops, and reported the matter to the police.

The Direct Investigation Group for Aerial Phenomena (DIGAP) began investigating the case under the supervision of Arthur Tomlinson and interviewed Shelley. All were convinced by her sincerity. In any case, where someone is affected in any way while in the vicinity of a UFO it draws particular interest, and the DIGAP members did wonder if the grinding sensation experienced by Shelley could have been caused by ultrasonic sound emitted by the object she witnessed.

The Treleigh School Sighting

At midday on 9 July 1976, three staff and around ninety children at Treleigh Primary School, Redruth, Cornwall, watched in amazement from their school yard as they saw a white, spinning, flying saucer surrounded by an 'aura or halo' in the sky. Teacher Deborah Foster was among those who saw it high in the sky as it came from Truro and passed out of sight over Carn Brea. Fellow teacher Sam Hawkins stated he had seen silver and yellow flashes at 90 degrees to the object's direction, adding it was travelling slowly and they could even see it when it passed through cloud. School secretary Sylvia Harris also saw the object and the flashes, which she described as 'like lightening and were spasmodic'. Pupils said the 'saucer' took on a greenish hue when it passed through the clouds, it bore no markings and did not appear to emit any sound.

The Fencehouses Enigma

At 9 p.m. on the dry and cool evening of 3 September 1976, two women, one aged sixty-three and the other eighteen (names withheld at their request), were walking home after visiting a friend in the colliery village of Fencehouses, near Sunderland in County Durham, when they had a truly bizarre experience with a UFO.

As they passed some wasteland a strange object caught their eye and, feeling somehow 'attracted towards it', they walked over to investigate. What they saw was an oval object resting on a mound of earth. The women estimated the object to be about 3 feet high and 5 feet long and it was standing on what appeared to be chrome or steel runners. The main compartment was glass-like with an orange-coloured section on top.

When they reached the object, the older woman recalled the noise of the street and traffic appeared to stop. She touched the glass-like sides of it and they felt warm. Suddenly, two strange beings appeared within it under the glass. They had long white hair parted down the middle, large eyes and claw-like hands. They appeared to be about the same size as large dolls, and were very much alive and seemed frightened at the sight of the ladies.

Both of the ladies were also frightened at what they had just seen and hurried away. As they did so, the sounds of street and traffic returned to their ears. The object then took off at great speed, emitting only a humming noise as it did so. The women estimated their encounter lasted approximately ten minutes and were left badly shaken by the experience. The area of land where the encounter occurred has since been redeveloped.

The Winchester Encounter

Joyce Bowles of Winchester was driving her Mini Clubman along the A272 Alton Road out of Winchester with family friend Ted Pratt on the evening of 14 November 1976. She only had to drive a handful of miles to Chilcomb to pick up her son from Chilcomb Farm where he had been visiting his girlfriend. As they were driving along the main road at 8.55 p.m. Joyce and Ted both spotted a bright orange-glowing light in the sky to the left of their car. The light disappeared soon after but was spotted again by Mrs Bowles when it started to hover low behind some trees a short distance further along the road. Several other people in the local area also confirmed that they had seen the same light that night. After travelling about a quarter of a mile they took the sharp left turn off, driving down Chilcomb Lane at about 20–25 miles per hour. Suddenly the car seemed to go out of control, veering to the right. Mr Pratt stated the engine 'went crazy' and started to shudder and shake.

They hit the wide grass verge and as Joyce grappled to regain control of the steering wheel, Mr Pratt took hold of it. Suddenly the car straightened itself and carried on down the grass verge for about 15 yards, then abruptly stopped. Both Joyce and Ted felt as if they had hit some sort of invisible barrier that stopped the car. At this point they saw a cigar-shaped object hovering in front of them that appeared to be resting on gas jets or vaporised steam that was blowing out from several points underneath. Joyce estimated the craft was 15 feet long.

Visible inside the craft were three humanoids dressed in silver overalls in what appeared to be a cockpit with a large, curved window which was lit up (but was not glowing) at the end of the 'cigar'.

One of the figures moved away from the others. It suddenly appeared through the mist formed by the vapour jets and began walking towards Joyce's side of the car. As this happened she recalls hearing a whistle, rather like that of a whistling kettle. The humanoid, which she estimated to be a tall man of just over 6 feet, had a close-cropped full beard and was wearing something like a boiler suit with a polo neck collar and only a seam down the right-hand side. The figure came to Joyce's window on the driver's side, put its arm on the roof of the car and looked in. She was struck by his 'entirely pink eyes, like an albino rabbit' that were very piercing.

The humanoid then cast its eyes at Joyce and Ted and around the interior of the car, then all of a sudden the car's engine sprung back into life. Joyce noticed, however, that the keys in the ignition had not been turned and her car headlight beams were four times more powerful than normal. The humanoid then walked around the car clockwise, passing around the back of the car, and looked as if he would approach Ted on the passenger side. Mr Pratt made to get out of the car but was held back and prevented from doing so by Joyce. Suddenly, the figure was no longer there, and neither was the hovering cigar-shaped UFO.

Joyce and Ted were both shaken but Mrs Bowles was determined she would not get out of the car so Ted could take over driving. Putting the car into gear, it seemed as if the invisible barrier was still holding the car back. Joyce slipped it into neutral and waited for a few moments, then put it back in gear and drove off, the car behaving as if nothing had happened. On the following Monday morning when she rose to start her day Joyce had a blotchy rash on her face, down her neck and across her shoulder on the right of her body – the same side the figure had been closest to.

In an interview for a TV documentary featuring Joyce and Ted, Mrs Bowles stated that she had been contacted by telephone by an official from London who told her that on no account was she to say anything to anyone about what they had seen because she was going to have a government official come round to see her. Adamant that England is a country of free speech, Joyce Bowles told her story 'because it is the truth'.

The Broad Haven Landing

The children of Broad Haven Primary School, Dyfed, West Wales, were out on the playing field enjoying lunch hour on Friday 4 February 1977 when about fourteen of the children aged between nine and eleven claimed they saw a flying saucer that was partially obscured by shrubbery in a field approximately 300 yards from their school. Generally, the children described a silvery cigar-shaped object (or a saucer viewed from the side) with a dome on top about the size of a bus. Some of the children also mentioned hearing a humming noise.

Six of the children also saw a humanoid creature near the craft which they described as being in a silver-grey suit the same colour as the saucer, and appeared to have elongated ears. David Ward (ten) added: He wasn't a very tall person, and he didn't look very nice either.' The children rushed inside and asked headmaster Ralph Llewellyn to come and see it but he refused. The children claimed the saucer seemed to disappear and reappear. It was spotted by more children during the afternoon and immediately after school. Despite not being willing to see the object for himself, the headmaster could see that the children had been shocked by something they had seen, so he separated them and asked them to draw what they saw. There were slight variations, but essentially they were all drawing very similar things.

The incident was investigated by retired veterinary surgeon Randall Jones Pugh, who was at that time the BUFORA area co-ordinator and a correspondent for UFOIN. Mr Pugh had been notified by the mother of David Davies (ten) of Tiers Cross who contacted him after her son had returned from school claiming to have seen a flying saucer. He began his investigation the same day and went to interview David, and from then onwards conducted a very thorough investigation of the incident.

Despite coverage in the local and national television, including John Craven's *Newsround* and *Swap Shop*, and press, including a special feature in the *Observer Magazine*, the sticking point was that despite the children being earnest in their claims (and many of their parents felt strongly that their child would not have made it up), no adult witnesses came to see what the children claimed to have seen. Consequently, some commentators were quick to dismiss the incident as the product of the overactive imaginations of the children.

Mr Pugh's research, however (published as a report for *Flying Saucer Review*, Vol. 23, No. 1, June 1977), revealed a female teacher at the school who wished to remain anonymous claimed she saw something when she left the school by the side entrance on 17 February 1977. It was pouring with rain at the time but something glinted and caught her attention in a nearby field, approximately 200 yards away. There, she saw a large oval-shaped object the colour of shining metal that had a slight dome. There was a humming noise and she watched the object glide off to the left.

Randall Jones Pugh went on to write *The Dyfed Enigma* (1979) with journalist Frederick William Holiday in which they recounted the numerous UFO sightings in the area dubbed the 'Dyfed Triangle' between 1974 and 1977. Over subsequent years claims have been made to have 'solved' the mystery by suggesting what the children had actually seen was a council sewage wagon, but the children who witnessed this event have now grown up, and several have been interviewed again over the years since the incident and remain convinced that they saw a UFO.

UFO Auto Stop Near Nelson, Lancashire

On the evening of 9 March 1977, Brian Grimshaw was driving his 1968 Vauxhall Viva with his friend Jeff (surname withheld at request). Both were employed on the night shift at a Nelson menswear factory and were on their way back to work after having dropped off a canteen assistant. Passing over this rather bleak and industrial landscape, with the Pennine Hills looming up around them, Jeff spotted a bright light in a low cloud in the sky over Pendle Hill. The light then dropped out of the clouds; it appeared to be a round ball of light. It hovered for a few seconds then started to move towards their car at what Brian estimated was about 5 mph. As the UFO got closer, the car lost gradually more power until, when the object was a short distance away, it came to a standstill. Brian put on the handbrake and the pair got out of the car to watch the UFO as it came ever closer.

The form of the UFO that had shone brightly could now be discerned as 'like a cigar with pointed end coloured shiny black against a dark sky'. The size of the UFO was judged by both witnesses to be bigger than a double-decker bus. There was an array of lights on the underside, two strange features that looked like oil drums attached to the extremities of the craft, oval windows on the front side and nothing on the back. Brian described them as 'thousands of them [lights] ... they just seemed to be moving. They were not all going in a straight line. They were all different ... the red and the orange stood out a lot'. The UFO was also surrounded by a grey mist that went to the edges of the object but did not cover it.

The UFO ended up directly overhead emitting a sound 'like the tide coming in and out'. As it hovered there Brian and Jeff felt a huge pressure or force bearing down upon them. At that point the pair just wanted to get away, but the car simply would not start; even the ignition light did not come on. After hovering for a few minutes, the UFO moved off slowly towards Manchester. The entire encounter lasted around ten minutes. When the UFO had gone the car restarted, and the pair arrived at the factory where they worked at 3.20 a.m. but both men were left with severe headaches and a pounding sensation in their foreheads.

The Hainault Forest Incident

At 3.55 a.m. on 3 May 1977 police received a 999 call from a public telephone box from someone who gave his name as David Samuels, who reported seeing a strange object near the lake at Hainault Forest in Essex. PC Bill Hefferman from Barkingside and a colleague from Chadwell Heath were despatched in a patrol car to attend the scene. The area in question is far more of a recreation area of parkland, and its gates are locked at night. At 4.12 a.m. the police entered using a duplicate key and began to travel up the small road just off the B196 Romford road that leads into the grounds. As they drove in they noticed a large, bright red light on the eastern side to the lake. The police officers stopped the car and got out so they could get a better look at the object. At this point the object was estimated to be 300 yards away from the police officers. It was red in colour (as bright as a car brake light) and of a shape and size similar to a bell tent and was hovering a short distance off the ground. It glowed and pulsated all the time it was in vision. As the police officers watched, the object seemed to 'dissolve on the spot'.

The officers decided to split up and search the area. While doing this, one of the officers noticed a strange white inverted-crescent object in the sky directly above the park, but he found himself struck dumb at the sight and could only alert his colleague after this UFO also dissolved into the darkness. The officers found no clues as to what these objects were at the site, but both noted a strong smell of burning confined to the eastern side of the lake. When the area was investigated shortly afterwards by Barry M. King of UFOIN, he found a large gorse bush at the back of the lake that had suffered recent extensive damage, 'looking as though a large and heavy weight had been placed in its central area'. In an intriguing twist to the story Barry's brother and fellow UFO researcher Steven was contacted by a gentleman who wanted to share his story. He had parked his car in the car park of a pub about half a mile away from the recreation ground, on the other side of the forest, near the area known as 'the Swamps', on the night of 8 May 1977. After his attention had been drawn by the sounds of movement in the bushes he saw an 8-foot-tall, dark-blue figure emerge that was 'brighter than its surroundings' and resembled a human in outline but had no obvious arms nor legs.

The witness agreed to be interviewed by Barry, but sadly he did not turn up and the trail for this element to the story sadly went cold, but this was not the last of UFO sightings over Hainault Forest that year.

According to a report in the Ilford newspaper *The Recorder* published in early August more than a dozen people had spotted a light in the sky that 'glowed menacingly over the forest area'. The most dramatic sighting occurred at 2 a.m. on Friday 29 July 1977 when husband and wife Terry and Maureen McCreanor of Rush Green were driving back home along Forest Road, Hainault, after a party.

Suddenly there was a 'flash of light' above the sports ground. Two lights materialised from the flash and began following the McCreanors' car. Maureen told a reporter: 'I was terrified. The lights just kept on following us.' The couple tried to take evasive action to lose the lights, and even diverted through back streets, but to no avail. By the time they arrived on Whalebone Lane in Dagenham they decided to pull in at the police station and alert them to the lights. A number of police officers on early morning duty joined the couple on the street and all witnessed the lights as they hovered in the sky. The lights eventually faded away, leaving everyone baffled at what they had just seen.

Mysterious 'Airship' Over the East Coast

During the night of Sunday 31 January 1978, a mysterious UFO was spotted off the east coast of England from the Tyne to Norfolk. It was even reported by pilots flying over the area on their way to Amsterdam. Two simultaneous sightings were made from coastguards at Cromer in Norfolk and from Skegness in Lincolnshire. Coastguards H. V. Brown and Colin Handforth were on duty at Cromer and observed the UFO through high-powered observation equipment for approximately thirty seconds. Mr Brown described what he saw: 'At first it looked like a big light and then an airship. It came just opposite us about two or three miles out, over the sea. It looked 200 yards long with bands of whitish light coming off in all directions. It looked like a spaceship.'

A spokesman from HM Coastguard rescue headquarters at Gorleston confirmed sightings had been reported to them, adding: 'It had a line of red and green lights down the side and something like a bright glow surrounded it. It was between one and three miles from the coast and its height estimated at 800-1000 feet ... it was so clear the coastguard thought it was a Boeing 707 with all its lights on.' This, however, was discounted when the air-traffic control centre at West Drayton, Middlesex, confirmed no civil nor military aircraft were in the area at the time.

The Dechmont Woods Incident

For foreman forester Robert 'Bob' Taylor (sixty-one) Friday 9 November 1979 was going to be just like any other day at work for the forestry section of the Livingston Development Corporation Estates Department where he had been employed for the past sixteen years. He said his goodbyes to his wife, Mary, from their home at Deans, climbed into his Bedford pick-up truck with his Irish setter dog, Lara, and made the short drive to Dechmont Wood, which is not far from the M8 motorway near Livingston New Town, West Lothian, Scotland, where he had planned to check on the fences and gates at the new forest plantations.

Arriving at the wood mid-morning, he parked up and walked up the track with his dog at his side. Bob rounded the corner into a clearing on the north side of Deer Hill when he was confronted by the sight of a 30-foot-high 'dome-shaped' object of a dark-grey metallic material with a rough texture, like sandpaper. Hardly able to believe what he was seeing, he tried to take in the features of the object, noting its upper section was ringed by regularly spaced dark circular areas or porthole-like apertures and was girdled by a rim or 'flange' of larger dimensions with what appeared to be metal 'stems' or cylindrical bars pointing vertically with small rotors on top.

As he stood there, Bob was suddenly aware of two spherical 'sea mine'-like objects of the same colour as the main ship about 3 feet in diameter with around six spike legs on each that made a sucking or popping sound as each contacted the ground and rolled towards him. These objects moved in unison and were on him in seconds. They 'fell' onto his sides and the spikes gripped his trousers and began dragging him towards the main ship. Bob fought hard against them, but they increased their grip. He could feel his wellington boots dragging along the ground and became aware of a foul, choking smell 'like burning brakes'. Bob fought on, feeling a pressure and burning sensation under his chin, then lost consciousness fell forward onto the grass.

Bob was aware of the sound of his dog, Lara, racing around him barking and a strange 'whooshing' sound occurred as he regained consciousness, but when he came round and looked around, the ship and the 'sea mines' were all gone. Dazed and confused, he crawled about 100 metres on his hands and knees before he could stagger to his feet and make it back to his pick-up truck where he attempted to report what had happened to his office on his two-way radio. Bob made contact but found he was unable to speak. He got into the driving seat of his truck and managed to start the engine, but he was still so disorientated he reversed it into a ditch.

Robert got out and resolved to try and walk home. As he did so, his senses began to return to him and his voice came back. Robert's wife recalled how Bob looked terrible when he came in the door of their home: his face was ashen and dirty, as were his clothes, and there was a red mark under his chin and jaw. She then noticed his trousers were torn. She asked if he had been in an accident with his lorry? Robert replied no, he had been attacked. 'By men?' she enquired, 'No, a spaceship thing.' he replied. Mary was incredulous; she thought he must have had a fall and hit his head and said she would call their family doctor. Dr Gordon Adams of the Blackburn surgery made a house call to see Bob. He recalled how Bob was clearly shaken by his experience and he gave him a full check over but could only find abrasions on either side of Bob's hips where his trousers and long johns had been torn.

Mary also rang Bob's boss, forestry manager Robert Drummond, who went to investigate where the incident occurred. On the ground he found marks similar to caterpillar tracks found on bulldozers, along with indentations some 3 inches deep and at a slight angle, which suggested a very heavy object had been rested there. He radioed for a team of his men to lay sheep net wire and posts around the area to prevent damage by passers-by and telephoned the police at Livingston.

Lothian and Borders Police took the matter seriously, treating it as a reported assault, with Chief Superintendent David Scott leading the enquiry. Detective Constable Ian Wark was part of the investigation, and he recalls arriving at the clearing and seeing the strange 'caterpillar track' impressions in the ground rather like the marks of two ladders, which were 10 feet long and 1 foot wide and 7 feet 8 inches apart.

Additionally, he noted approximately forty circular impressions in the ground, each one measuring about 3.5 inches in diameter. He also photographed and made a sketch of the marks on the ground. Significantly, the tracks he had seen did not appear anywhere other than the clearing where Bob had been attacked: 'They did not come from anywhere or go anywhere. They just arrived as though a helicopter or something had landed from the sky.'

PC William Douglas also saw the tracks and made a wide sweep of the area, noting it was very soft due to recent rain so would remain for some time, but still found no tracks beyond, indicating whatever had caused the tracks had been driven or towed away, and would have to report he could find 'no rational explanation' for the marks.

In an attempt to resolve the mystery, DC Wark went to the Livingston Development Corporation depot to see if he could match the tracks to any of their machinery but found no matches. Bob's ripped trousers and long johns were also sent for examination at the Lothian and Borders Police Forensic Science Laboratory in Edinburgh. Sadly, the incident occurred before DNA testing, but their examination did reveal the damage to the trousers was consistent with having been damaged by 'a mechanical type of action' hooking on or grabbing the trousers and tearing of the fabric. The long johns reflected similar damage. None of the damage was typical of a snag on a tree branch, thorns or barbed wire, nor was it due to Bob falling to the ground.

This story made national headlines and has featured on numerous tv and radio documentaries over the years. Anyone who knew Robert Taylor, a father of five children, a veteran of both the Dunkirk evacuation and the Normandy campaign who saw active service as a tank driver in the Fife and Forfar Yeomanry during the Second World War and a respected member of his local community, knew he was not a man likely to invent such a story. In fact, he candidly said he was doubtful he would have believed the story if he had not seen it himself. Despite telling it many times until his death aged eighty-eight in March 2007, Bob never varied his story and it has entered into local legend. A commemorative plaque to mark the site where the encounter took place was erected in 1992 but was stolen so many times that the council stopped replacing it. In 2018 a waymarked UFO trail recalling the events of that fateful November morning in 1979 was opened in Dechmont Woods. Today the Dechmont Woods incident is claimed to be the only reported UFO incident to become the subject of a formal investigation by British police.

Chapter 6

The 1980s and 1990s

The Mystery of Zygmund Adamski

At 3.45 p.m. on the afternoon of 11 June 1980 the body of a middle-aged man was discovered by Trevor Parker on top of a 10-foot coal pile at his father's coal yard in Todmorden, West Yorkshire. The body was identified as that of expatriate Polish coal miner Zygmund Jan Adamski (fifty-six). The post-mortem conducted later that day noted he was 5-foot 6-inches tall and weighed approximately 10 stones. He had consumed no food for twelve hours before he died. He had one day's growth of beard and was wearing a suit, but it seemed as if it had been hastily put back on him as it was incorrectly fastened; his shirt, wallet and watch were missing. The body did not exhibit any signs to suggest he had been sleeping rough and there was no sign of foul play. Cause of death was recorded as 'heart attack'. The estimated time of death was given as eight to ten hours before the body was discovered. The coroner would record an open verdict.

There were, however, some deeply puzzling factors about this case. Mr Adamski lived over 20 miles away in Tingley, near Wakefield. He had a stable, quiet family life. He cared for his wife, Lottie, had no major worries and had been looking forward to giving his goddaughter away at her wedding on 7 June. He had last been seen as he popped out from his home to the shops to buy some groceries on 6 June.

Mr Adamski had been missing for five days but he had died only hours before he was found. His hair had also been cropped very short in what was described as a 'roughly cut' manner. He had died with his eyes wide open and staring, which suggests at the moment of death he had been in terror. His body had been 'exposed to water' after his death and he had suffered a non-fatal burn caused by a corrosive liquid that had been applied to his head, neck and shoulders.

The strangest element of all is how does a man who died some hours before he was discovered on the top of a 20-foot-high coal heap end up there? Men had been working on the heap on the morning before the body was discovered; they had certainly not noticed any body lying on top of it, and there were no clues to indicate how he got there. The tip had been seen empty hours after the time of Mr Adamski's death, so it would have been impossible for him to have crawled up there himself and it would have taken time and have been very difficult for anyone to scale the slippery coal heap hauling a body with them unseen in broad daylight. It was hardly a discreet site to dump a body.

At the inquest it was suggested the obvious answer to the conundrum was that the body had been placed where it had been found from above. The front page of the *Sunday Mirror* pulled no punches and declared the case an 'Amazing UFO Death Riddle'. PC Alan Godfrey, who was the first police officer on the scene after the discovery of Mr Adamski's body, shared the opinion that Mr Adamski had been abducted by aliens and had been placed on the coal heap by some means after he died of the heart attack. PC Godfrey would have his own encounter with a UFO later that same year (see 'The Todmorden Encounter', p. 131).

The Earsdon Incident

On 21 August 1980, housewife Lillian Middleton (thirty-three) was driving late at night along the road between Earsdon and her home at Tillmouth Avenue, Holywell, near Seaton Delaval, Whitley Bay, Northumberland. Although not a remote area, the land between the villages is large, open agricultural fields. As she drove along, Lillian became aware of an unidentified flying object emitting a brilliant light hovering above the roof of her car, which she had to travel at speeds of up to 70 mph to escape. Speaking on behalf of his traumatised wife, John Middleton told reporters: 'This really terrified her. Neither of us has ever had the car go faster than 50mph but she was so shocked that she just wanted to get away. I am keeping an open mind but my wife is not trying to invent things. She said that the object was as big as her car and at times was almost touching the roof. It had a brilliant white light but every time she stopped the car it zoomed back into the air and hovered above.'

A police spokesman stated: 'We are treating this seriously because number of different people saw the same thing. At one time quite few people at an all-night garage were watching this object.' Mr Middleton concluded: 'Although it has not put my wife off driving it will be a long time before she goes out on her own at night.'

The Wetherby Wonder

The Yorkshire Post reported West and North Yorkshire Police had been chasing a UFO early on Saturday 13 September 1980. The object described as a bright diamond-shaped light was first seen by police officers near Wetherby, West Yorkshire. A West Yorkshire police spokesman said: 'Altogether, five officers saw this object and described it as brighter and larger than any star. PC Roy Allen and PC Richard Gordon had been alerted in York that the object was heading towards their patrol car.'

PC Allen recounted: 'We were on the York bypass when suddenly we saw it. The light stopped moving and hovered in the sky for some time. Eventually it moved off in the direction of Hull.'

Police checked with local RAF stations and RAF Fylingdales, but no satisfactory explanation of the UFO was offered. The army was carrying out a Home Defence Exercise in the north at the same time, but a spokesman stated that he knew of nothing that could account for what was sighted. A senior police officer at York commented: 'There is nothing we can do. It has been logged as an unidentified flying object.' Humberside police also stated that an 'oval shaped, pinky red' UFO had also been sighted and reported by teenagers shortly before 10 p.m. on Saturday night.

The Todmorden Encounter

PC Alan Godfrey (thirty-three) was out in his Ford Escort patrol car in rural West Yorkshire on 28 November 1980 and looking forward to his shift coming to an end when at 5.15 a.m. he received a call to attend an estate on Burnley Road where thirty cows were reported to be roaming free. Unable to locate any cattle, he was just completing a final circuit before heading back to his station. As he was turning off the A646, the main Burnley to Todmorden road, he spotted a strange glow about 200 yards away and went to investigate.

As he drove along the road he was confronted by what appeared to be a large, bright, almost diamond-shaped object hovering about 5 feet over the centre of the road. When approximately 100 yards from the object, the lights of his patrol car began to reflect off its shiny white surface. PC Godfrey stopped his vehicle and took in what he was seeing. It did not cross his mind at that time that what he was seeing might be a spaceship; he was just wondering what it was, what it was doing there and was mindful of what might happen if another vehicle was coming the other way down the road.

The thing he was looking at was diamond shaped with a flatter top than its base. It was about 14 feet high and approximately 20 feet wide; in fact, it spanned the width of the road and hovered above it, while the lights of his police car shone underneath it. Fluorescent light emanated from the top of the craft, and he could see a row of dark, square windows beneath the light. The top portion remained static while the bottom rotated clockwise at a fantastic speed. As he observed the scene, he noted that despite there being no breeze that morning the leaves on trees around the object were blowing around as if caught by a strong wind.

Alan tried to radio in what he was seeing, but found his car radio was dead – there was not even static registering. He reached for his personal walkie-talkie and found that was dead too. Thinking quickly, he grabbed his clipboard and set about drawing a sketch of what he was seeing. Suddenly, he looked up from the board to see a brilliant, dazzling, white light.

The next thing he was aware of, PC Godfrey was driving his car another 30 or 40 yards down the road from where he had encountered the strange craft. He had no recollection of how this had happened. Shaken by his experience, Alan looked in the mirror to see if the object was still there or if it had gone. There was no sign of it. He then turned his car around and went back to the scene, but there was nothing there. He still stopped his patrol car and looked behind just in case.

Alan set off to drive to his police station in Todmorden but spotted a colleague in another patrol car. He flagged him down and told him what he had seen. Alan and his colleague drove back to the scene in their respective patrol cars to see if there was any evidence of the nocturnal visitor left behind. They found the spot deserted, with nothing other than oily patches on the road surface and 'whirlpool-shaped marks' on the damp road immediately beneath where the object had been hovering.

It was also at this time the other officer noticed a split in Alan's boot, which looked very much as if it had been dragged along the ground. Alan was pretty sure it had not been like that at the start of his shift, and he could not recall any time since that it could have happened. When he later took his boot off, he found a strange itchy mark on his foot. PC Godfrey's story hit the local and national press. He was also quizzed by UFO investigators and a senior police officer, and it was during this questioning it became apparent that PC Godfrey could not account for about forty minutes of the night he saw the UFO.

Alan underwent hypnotic regression, during which he recalled being abducted. PC Godfrey spoke of experiencing a floating sensation and waking up in a room in which he felt compelled to lay on a bed. Around him were frightening smaller beings that were about 3-foot 6-inches high with dark eyes that attached something to his ankle. He could also recall a humanoid creature with a beard being present.

The Rendlesham Forest Incident – Britain's Roswell

The 'twin bases' of RAF Bentwaters and RAF Woodbridge were both constructed late during the Second World War, in 1943. The pair are only a short distance apart, with Rendlesham Forest, heath and farmland between and around them in rural Suffolk. Although built for the RAF, the control of both bases was transferred to the USAF in 1951 and they were used as fighter bases from the 1950s to the 1990s. It is also believed that nuclear weapons were stored at Woodbridge air base in the 1980s when, at the height of the Cold War, such bases were at a constant readiness in the event of attack by the Soviets, so it is hardly surprising that military personnel involved in the security of the airfields at that time were both well trained and vigilant.

The extraordinary events that took place in Rendlesham Forest between 26 and 28 December 1980 set the base abuzz with rumours, but these were played down and the security around it was tight. Still, tales of something having happened reached the ears of local people. Some locals had witnessed the mysterious lights themselves, while some even believed an aircraft had crashed into the forest and sought answers about what they had seen. A late news item revealing that there were rumours of 'at least one major UFO event' involving United States Air Force personnel from RAF Bentwaters air base at Rendlesham Forest by Jenny Randles, dated 21 February 1981, was published in the next available edition of *Flying Saucer Review*.

In a second article for a later edition that same year, Jenny built on what was then known and related the sterling efforts of Brenda Butler and Dot Street to investigate and get to the truth of what had happened. The world, however, would have to wait for almost three years for the story to fully break in the British national press when an American serviceman (identified in the article under a false name) told what he knew to the *News of the World*, which duly carried the front-page headline 'UFO Lands in Suffolk and That's Official' on 2 October 1983.

The events at Rendlesham Forest have become the subject of numerous books, articles and documentaries over the years since. Some extraordinary claims have been made, but few are left in doubt that something extraordinary happened in Rendlesham Forest forty-five years ago. The incident has rightly become known as 'Britain's Roswell'.

A Suffolk Police form records a message received from A1C Arnold at the Law Enforcement Desk, Bentwaters, at 4.11 a.m. on 26 December 1980, which stated: 'We have a sighting of some unusual lights in the sky, we have sent some unarmed troops to investigate, we are terming it as a UFO at present.' The form notes the location given as 'beyond East Gate to RAF Woodbridge'. By the time the police attended the scene there was nothing to see: 'Air Traffic Control at West Drayton checked, no knowledge of aircraft. Reports received of aerial phenomena over southern England during the night. Only lights visible [in] this area was from Orford Lighthouse use. Search made of area negative.'

The negative return has been cited several times by more than one researcher as 'proof' nothing happened or that it was all a mistake, arguing that Orford Lighthouse was the real source of the lights seen by the members of the Woodbridge security police on 26 December and, ultimately, Lieutenant Colonel Charles Halt and the team he took out to investigate the mysterious lights in the forest on the night of 27/28 December. If this had been the case, though, surely the light shone by the lighthouse would have been seen before and therefore recognised for what is was by those on base and easily dismissed as nothing to be concerned about. Accounts of the moving and splitting lights witnessed by those who were there simply do not seem typical of the beam of light, nor the colours of the lights shone from a lighthouse.

The following account is based on the 'Unexplained Lights' memorandum Halt drew up about the events which he submitted to the Ministry of Defence in January 1981. Colonel Halt dates events starting on 27 December on the memo, but, as will be shown, the lights were first sighted on 26 December. I also draw on the witness statements taken in the immediate aftermath of the incident from those who witnessed and experienced the events personally.

At approximately 3 a.m. during the early hours of 26 December 1980, USAF security police patrol men Staff Sergeant Bud Steffens and A1C John Burroughs saw unusual lights outside the east gate (sometimes referred to as the back gate) at RAF Woodbridge. Burroughs recalled:

> ...while on patrol down at east gate myself and my partner saw lights coming from the woods due east of the gate. The lights were red and blue, the red one above the blue one, they were flashing on and off. Because I've never seen anything like that coming from the woods before we decided to drive down and see what it was. We went down east gate road and took a right at the stop sign and drove down about 10 to 20 yards to where there is a road that goes into the forest. At the road we could see a white light shimmering onto the trees and I could still see the red and blue lights. We decided we better call it in...

So, the pair then made their way back to the east gate, keeping an eye on the lights as they did so. Some researchers have suggested that what the USAF witnesses saw was in fact the lights of a UK police car, but the Suffolk Police log shows they were not contacted until 4.11 a.m. – over an hour after Burroughs and his partner first sighted the lights.

Lieutenant Fred Buran was on duty at Building 679, Central Security Control, and recalled SSgt Jim Penniston and his rider A1C Ed Cabansag were radioed to attend Steffens and Burroughs at the east gate. On arrival, SSgt Penniston confirmed that he too could see the lights reported by Burroughs. In his statement Buran noted: 'SSgt Penniston also reported the strange lights. I directed SSgt Coffey, the on-duty Security Controller, to attempt to ascertain from SSgt Penniston whether or not the lights could be marker lights of some kind to which SSgt Penniston said that he had never seen lights of this colour or nature in the area before. He described them as red, blue, white and orange. SSgt Penniston requested permission to investigate. After he had been joined by the Security Flight Chief, MSgt Chandler, and turned his weapon over to him, I directed them to go ahead.'

SSgt Penniston, A1C Burroughs and A1C Ed Cabansag then set off into the forest to investigate. SSgt Jim Penniston explains what happened next in his statement:

> Upon arriving at east gate directly to the east about 1½ miles in a large wooded area a large yellow glowing light was emitting above the trees. In the centre of the lighted area, there was a red light blinking on and off at 5 to 10 second intervals and a blue light that was being for the most part steady. After receiving permission from CSC, we proceeded off base past east gate, down an old logging road. Left vehicle and proceeded on foot. Burroughs and I were approx. 15-20 meters apart

and proceeding on a true east direction from the logging road. The area in front of us was lighting up a 30-metre area. When we got within a 50-metre distance the object was producing red and blue light. The blue light was steady and projecting under the object. It was lighting up the area directly under and extending a metre or two out. At this point of positive identification I relayed to CSC, SSgt Coffey. Positive sighting of the object ... 1 ... colour of lights and that it was definitely mechanical in nature. This is the closest I was near the object at any point. We then proceeded after it. On the way back we encountered a blue streaking light to left lasting only a few seconds. After a 45-minute walk we arrived at our vehicle.

Lieutenant Fred Buran had monitored the radioed report of Penniston, Burroughs and Cabansag as they entered the wooded area:

> They appeared to be very close to the lights, and at one point SSgt Penniston stated that it was a definute mechanical object. Due to the colours they had reported I alerted them to the fact that they may have been approaching a light aircraft crash scene. I directed SSgt Coffey to check with the tower to see if they could throw some light on the subject. They could not help.
>
> SSgt Penniston reported getting near the 'object' and then all of a sudden said they had gone past it and were looking at a marker beacon that was in the same general direction as the other lights. I asked him through SSgt Coffey if he could have been mistaken, to which Penniston replied that had I seen the other lights I would know the difference. SSgt Penniston seemed somewhat agitated at this point.
>
> They continued to look further, to no avail. At approximately 0354 hours, I terminated the investigation and ordered all units back to their normal duties. I directed SSgt Penniston to take notes of the incident when he came in that morning. After talking with him face to face concerning the incident, I am convinced that he saw something out of the realm of explanation for him at that time. I would like to state at this time that SSgt Penniston is a totally reliable and mature individual. He was not overly excited, nor do I think he is subject to overreaction or misinterpretation of circumstances. Later that morning, after conversing with Captain Mike Verano, the day shift commander, I discovered there had been several other sightings.

Having spoken to the witnesses, Halt summarised and enlarged on the details of the events in the forest in his memorandum:

> The individuals reported seeing a strange glowing object in the forest. The object was described as being metallic in appearance and triangular in shape, approximately two or three metres across the base and approximately two metres high. It illuminated the entire forest with a white light. The object itself had a pulsating red light on top and a bank of blue lights underneath. The object was hovering or on legs. As the patrol-men approached the object, it manoeuvred through the trees and disappeared. At this time the animals on a nearby farm went into a frenzy. The object was briefly sighted approximately an hour later near the back gate. The next day three depressions 1½ inches deep and 7 inches in diameter were found where the object had been sighted on the ground.

The following day, Saturday 27 December, rumours of what had happened the previous night spread like wildfire across the air base. Lieutenant Colonel Halt had heard the rumours and found what he heard hard to believe and was keen to debunk it. During the evening, lights were again seen in Rendlesham Forest. It was the officers' Christmas party on the base and Lieutenant Bruce England, the duty flight commander for the police, tracked down the base commander, Colonel Ted Conrad, at the event and quietly informed him that the UFO had returned. As host for the evening, Colonel Conrad was about to present awards and give a speech, so he asked Lieutenant Colonel Halt to deal with the situation.

Halt immediately sent a team from base security to set up 'light-alls' in the woods and called Sergeant Monroe Nevels, a Chemical Defence Instructor from the Disaster Preparedness team, to grab his camera (he was a professional photographer) and calibrate several Radiac instruments to take along. Halt then returned to his quarters at Bentwaters to change, joining his team in the forest shortly after midnight. Halt brought with him a hand-held Lanier micro-cassette recorder so that he could dictate notes as events unfolded. The recording that ensued is one of the most remarkable narratives relating to any UFO sighting.

Initial investigations in the forest centred around the landing site area where Penniston and Burroughs had reported seeing the strange craft. Upon Halt's arrival at the forest, he found what appeared to be a mechanical problem with the light-all and had to send back to base for another one. In the meantime, he organised readings to be taken with the Geiger counter. In his memorandum, Halt notes: 'The Beta/gamma readings of 0.1 milliroentgens were recorded with peak readings in the three depressions and near the centre of the triangle formed by the depressions. A nearby tree had moderate (.05 -.07) readings on the side of the tree toward the depressions.'

On the cassette tape, Lieutenant England can be heard pointing out to Halt that the trees around the landing site have abrasions on the bark of their trunks facing the centre of the area. Halt notes on the tape: 'The indentations look like something twisted as it dropped ... you know, as it sat down on them. Looks like someone took something and sat it down and twisted it from side to side. Very strange.' It is interesting to note that in his statement A1C Ed Cabansag noted when he spotted the lights in the forest with Penniston and Burroughs on 26 December: 'I saw a quick movement, it looked visible for a moment. It looked like it spun left a quarter of a turn, then it was gone.'

England also deployed a starlight (night-vision) scope and noted several of the trees at the landing site gave off 'a definite heat reflection' about 3 to 4 feet off the ground. Halt also noted: 'Looking directly overhead one can see an opening in the trees, plus some freshly broken pine branches on the ground underneath. Looks like some of 'em came off about 15 to 20 feet up. Some small branches about an inch or less in diameter.'

At 1.48 a.m. (now 28 December) Halt records: 'We're hearing very strange sounds out of the farmer's barnyard animals. They're very, very active, making an awful lot of noise.'

Shortly afterwards Lieutenant England spots a light between the trees and directs Halt's attention to it with the beam of this torch. Halt describes it for the tape: 'It's a strange, small red light, looks to be maybe a quarter to a half mile, maybe further out.' The light disappears, so Halt turns off his torch. Light then returns and he orders all torches out. The animals that were so restive are now quiet and still; in fact, the forest takes on an eerie silence.

The light soon returns, and it appears to Halt to be red with a tinge of yellow and brighter than before. It also appeared to be moving towards Halt and his men with particles of it shooting off as it did so, to which Halt exclaims, 'There is no doubt about it. This is weird!' A short while later the tape records:

> Halt: OK, we're looking at the thing, we're probably about two to three hundred yards away. It looks like an eye winking at you. Still moving

> from side to side. And when you put the Starscope on it, it sort of has a hollow centre, a dark centre, it's...
>
> England: Like a pupil...
>
> Halt: Yeah, like a pupil of an eye looking at you, winking. And the flash is so bright to the Starscope that it almost burns your eye.

In his memorandum, Halt described: 'a red sun-like light was seen through the trees. It moved about and pulsed'.

Halt and his men pursued the light to the edge of the forest and across a farmer's field. On the opposite side was a farm cottage that was illuminated by the powerful red glow of the UFO – it almost appeared as if it was on fire. In his memorandum, Halt recounts what happened next as the UFO '...then broke into five separate white objects and then disappeared'.

Halt would recall in a later interview for the *Unsolved Mysteries* series that when the UFO had divided there had been 'a very strange feeling in the air. It made your hair bristle, sort of like static electricity. You just had a very unusual feeling and don't think it was all psychological. I think there was something physiological about it.'

At 3.05 a.m. Halt and his team observed in the sky that there were 'strange, strobe-like flashes ... rather sporadic but there's definitely something there. Some kind of phenomenon'. In his memorandum, Halt describes:

> Immediately afterwards, three star-like objects were noticed in the sky, two objects to the north and one to the south, all of which were about 10 degrees off the horizon. The objects moved rapidly in sharp angular movements and displayed red, green and blue lights. The objects to the north appeared to be elliptical through an 8-12 power lens. They then turned to full circles. The objects to the north remained in the sky for an hour or more. The object to the south was visible for two or three hours and beamed down a stream of light from time to time.

One of the objects even came towards Halt and his team at a very high speed and a pencil beam came down onto the ground only a short distance from their feet. Halt he exclaims on his recording: 'This is unreal.'

Colonel Halt was of the opinion that the UFOs were under some form of intelligent control. Sgt Robert Ball of the base security police was with Colonel Halt watching the same lights. To Ball, they appeared 'as if they were conducting a grid search, boxing off an area and looking for something'.

Halt concludes his memo by pointing out that numerous individuals, including himself, had witnessed the events outlined in his memorandum. In a later interview, Halt added that personnel in the weapons storage area and in several other places on the base, even his immediate superior who was standing in his front yard at Woodbridge, could see the beams of light being projected down by the craft. From Colonel Holt's perspective, his memorandum was met with silence and the incidents were subject to a cover-up. Now retired, Colonel Halt candidly expresses his opinion that what he saw was extra-terrestrial. His view is shared by many of the others who witnessed those events in Rendlesham Forest in late December 1980.

Plymouth Woman Burned by UFO Beam

Accounts clerk Denise Bishop (twenty-three) was returning home to her parent's home in Weston Mill Hill, Plymouth, at 11.15 p.m. on Thursday 10 September 1981 when she noticed a strange light behind the bungalow. As she reached the door her view improved and she saw a huge UFO around 125 feet wide which she described as having the same shape and body of a crab. Taking in what she saw, Denise described:

> The object was unlit, and dark metallic grey, but coming from underneath it and shining down on the rooftops beneath it were six or seven broad shafts of light. These were in lovely pastel shades of pink and purple and there was also white. I saw all this in an instant, and I was terrified. I hurriedly reached the door, but as I put my hand on the handle, from the unlit side of the craft a lime-green-coloured pencil beam of light came down and hit the back of my hand. As soon as it touched my hand I couldn't move but was stopped dead in my tracks. The beam stayed on my hand for at least thirty seconds ... The green beam which gave off no illumination was rather like a rod of light then switched off and I continued to open the back door. It was as though a film had been stopped and then started again. I had been stopped in mid-stride and when the beam went off I continued with the same movement as before.

Denise opened the door and rushed inside, and as she did so the UFO lifted up slightly and moved off. When inside she told her sister what had happened and when she examined her hand there were spots of blood on it which she washed off and while she did so she saw a burn mark where the beam had been.

The Ilkley Moor Incident

Retired Police Officer Philip Spencer (a pseudonym used since the earliest publication of this story; the witness has maintained his anonymity to date) was walking over Ilkley Moor, Yorkshire, to take some exercise and visit his father-in-law at East Morton on 1 December 1987. The views from across the hills can be great so Philip had his camera with him. Despite the weather being windy and overcast Philip made good progress over the rocky terrain.

As Philip trekked along he spotted movement ahead of him. He could hardly believe his eyes for there was a dark-green creature, just 4ft tall with an oversized head and long, thin arms. The creature seemed to be aware of him and made a gesture that Philip interpreted as he should stay away but he managed to take a photograph of it then it then ran off. He tried to follow but the creature disappeared behind an outcrop and a 'whitish' flying saucer rose up from the moor emitting an intense hum and sped off.

Understandably shaken by the encounter, Philip headed to the nearest town of Ilkley, where he was soon to discover that having fully expected it to be 8.15 a.m. it was actually 10.00 a.m., almost two hours later than he expected it to be. Could he really have just lost nearly two hours? His compass also seemed to have had its polarity reversed.

Philip had the film from his camera developed soon afterwards. The small figure could be discerned on the image, but it was judged too grainy to be subjected to close scrutiny. The negatives were examined by experts from Kodak who confirmed there was no evidence of tampering. In March 1988 Philip agreed to undergo a session of regressive hypnotherapy during which he claimed he had been paralysed when he saw the creature, he was then levitated and taken on board the space craft that he had seen leave. When aboard the craft a medical examination had been carried out on him by a group of small green aliens. He was then shown disturbing films about disasters on the earth and threats like nuclear weapons. He was then returned to the moor.

The A70 Incident

On the evening of 17 August 1992, friends Garry Wood (thirty-three) and Colin Wright (twenty-five) were making a forty-minute journey along the A70 from Oxgangs, Edinburgh, to drop off a satellite system to a friend in the village of Tarbrax, south Lanarkshire. Garry was driving along at a steady 40 mph when, having just passed Harperrig Reservoir (about 9 miles from their destination), both Garry and Colin noticed a dark, disc-shaped object about 30 feet wide that was hovering 20 feet above the ground. They drove past the UFO, but it caught up in a flash and moved directly in front of their car. As they approached the UFO they could see that it appeared to be smooth, metallic, reflective and there were no apparent windows. As the pair drove under the craft it emitted a silver curtain of mist and light which they had no time to avoid.

Once inside the light was blinding but suddenly both men found themselves alone in a black void, no friend nearby, no car, no road. Garry recalled just standing looking around and wondering if he was dead and this was what death felt like. After what he thought was just fifteen seconds, the blinding light returned and Garry came round with a jolt to find the rear of their vehicle was crossing the centre of the road on a collision course with the embankment and he had to fight hard to regain control of the car.

Shaken, Garry stopped the car, and the pair took a moment to process what had just happened. They then carried on their journey to their friend in Tarbrax. When they arrived and knocked at his door they were both stunned to find their friend had gone to bed and was woken by their knocks at the door. They thought they were arriving around 10.30, but it turned out it was just after 12.45 a.m. Surely, they had only been unconscious for a second. Or had they really just 'lost time' somehow? They chatted amongst themselves through the night, wondering just what had happened, but Garry was convinced he did not have total recall of everything that had happened to him.

Over the following days both men were left feeling lethargic, suffering from headaches and insomnia; when Garry could get some sleep he was plagued by nightmares. Visiting his doctor, he was given a full examination, and no illness or injury could be found. Garry was also sent to a hospital where an MRI and a lumbar puncture were carried out in the hope of finding what was causing these ailments. No cause was found.

Garry and Kevin then agreed to try hypnotic regression. Both men's bodies convulsed as they recalled vague images and experiencing *something*. Over a number of sessions Garry and Colin began to recall how six small entities had come out of the craft and, dividing into two groups of three, removed Garry and Colin from the car. They had then been taken aboard the UFO where they were stripped naked, restrained and subjected to examinations and scans by the taller alien abductors. In a subsequent newspaper interview Garry is quoted describing them as around 6ft tall, '...white-grey in colour with a large head and dark eyes with a long, slender neck, very slim shoulders and waist. There were either ribs or folds of skin on its body. The arms were like ours, but there were four very long fingers'. After the examinations, they were then returned to their vehicle. Eerily, during their regression sessions, both Garry and Colin believed they saw other humans detained on the craft going through exactly the same examinations as them.

Recently declassified documents show the MoD undertook an investigation into the incident and an official report on it was filed in 1994, which suggested 'American military testing' which was occurring at the nearby RAF Kirknewton base at Whitemoss at the time as a possible cause.

The Cannock Chase Portal, 1993

Cannock Chase in Staffordshire, West Midlands, consists of a mixture of deciduous woodland, heathland and coniferous forest with waymarked pathways ideal for walking and mountain biking. It is a popular spot for family and friends outings all year round. Designated an Area of Outstanding Natural Beauty in 1958, covering just 26 square miles, it is the smallest area to be designated in mainland Britain, but from within it come a host of stories: eyewitness reports of hellhounds, a dogman who has even appeared on busy roads, cattle mutilations, a black-eyed young girl, UFOs and even a 7-foot-tall pig-faced man.

A reason suggested for the intensity of strange creatures in the area is that it may be a portal where creatures from other worlds or dimensions enter and exit ours. An incident that lends weight to this theory was witnessed by Brendan Davis Markshall in 1993. The spooky stories attached to the woods have quite a reputation among locals, especially teenagers, so when a couple of Brendan's friends passed their driving test they decided to venture out on a drive to the spooky woods at Cannock Chase after dark.

Finding a small gravel car park a short distance from the main parking area, they pulled in and parked up. Brendan points out they had not been drinking or smoking. They just sat in the cars, on the roof or on the bonnet chatting and messing about, as friends do, when what they assumed was an abnormally slow shooting star passed over their heads and disappeared into the trees in front of them.

They didn't think much more about it until they spotted a light moving towards them through the trees. Feeling increasingly disconcerted, when the light reached the treeline they turned the headlights of both cars on full beam to see who or what it was. The sight that met them was of some thirty or so people of all ages standing among the trees. Although they were all dressed in different attire, their clothes were not appropriate for a night hike through a forest.

Brendan and his friends were petrified. A man, who did not seem sinister in any way, then stepped forward from the group and asked in a friendly manner, 'Why don't you come over here.' The teenagers had seen enough; they dived into their cars and drove off.

Another UFO Over RAF Cosford

Thirty years after reports of a UFO landing at Cosford hit the newspapers (see 'UFO Landing at RAF Cosford', p. 78), another UFO made a dramatic appearance over RAF Cosford in Staffordshire at approximately 1.15 a.m. on 31 March 1993. An MoD police patrol reported seeing a huge triangular UFO with lights at the points of its extremities hovering at about 200 feet above the base. The craft was heard to emit a low humming noise and was seen to shoot out a beam of light down onto the ground beneath it before flying off at high speed in a south-east direction, leaving trails of luminous vapour behind it. No trace of the UFO was picked up on radar (officially, at least). Perhaps it used some kind of cloaking device?

Black Triangle Over Derbyshire

During the evening and night of 26 September 1993, a huge black triangle with three white corner lights and a large light in its centre was spotted by numerous people as it flew low, slow and silently over Derbyshire. There were multiple witnesses when the triangle made an appearance over the Bakewell/Matlock area at around 9.30 p.m. One was Mrs Hilda Hill, who drew a sketch of the triangle as it flew over her. Mrs Susan Shah, who resided on a hill overlooking Matlock Baths, saw bright lights approaching her house. After opening a window, she watched the massive triangle as it passed overhead.

Mrs Pailing of Bakewell also saw the triangle and noted that when she saw the UFO it had red, green and brilliant white lights. Mr Andrews was driving towards Bakewell when he first spotted slow-moving bright lights in the sky ahead of him and, as he entered the town, was struck by people looking up and watching a huge black triangle as it passed overhead. 'Lit up like a Christmas tree ... it had a very bright light at each corner, so bright that it illuminated the ground below.' It performed a series of manoeuvres, including 'U' turns and right-angle turns, before resuming its original course and slowly flying away.

Black Triangle Over Essex

A 'black triangle' described as 1.5 times the size of a football field was spotted flying along the seafront at Holland-on-Sea on Sunday 5 November 1993. Witnesses described how it had a variety of coloured lights underneath, a line of red lights at the rear, indentations on the underneath and a black circle in the centre. Another black triangle was spotted over the seafront at Clacton-on-Sea later that same month at 3.25 a.m. on 18 November 1993. Witnesses described a series of red and white lights along the two leading edges and a line of red lights along the rear edge. It moved slowly and silently, then suddenly 'took off like a rocket' but without the flame.

'Tic Tac' UFO Intercepted by RAF Jet Over Norfolk

It was dusk in early September 1996 and Neil Storey (twenty-four), the author of this book, was parked on a sugar beet pad on the high ground on Hagg Loke (now known as Field Lane), just off Yarmouth Road, North Walsham, Norfolk. Neil was with his girlfriend in her car and the pair were enjoying a snack as they watched the sun go down over the rolling Norfolk countryside. From their vantage point they could see for miles around across agricultural fields; even Happisburgh Lighthouse with its distinctive red and white rings 6 miles away could be seen by the naked eye on this fine, clear evening. As they sat enjoying the food and the view, a bright, glowing, white, elongated orb appeared in the sky and could be seen plainly moving at speed through the passenger door window as it passed over trees and flew at some considerable speed over the car, but so low it cast its glow over the dashboard as it did so.

Hardly believing their eyes, both got out of the car and watched the glowing object fly over to a treeline in the distance (about 1 mile away) where it paused then proceeded to move horizontally, steadily and smoothly from side to side just over the treetops. Neil kept the UFO in his vision and walked around the bonnet of the car to join his girlfriend on the driver's side to watch it, saying as he did so: 'If a fighter jet comes over there will certainly be something strange going on.' There were a few air bases in East Anglia where it could have come from in those days, including RAF Coltishall where Jaguar jet fighters were based just a few miles away. The words had barely left his lips before a jet fighter flew overhead and was heading on an interception course for the UFO. As the jet approached the UFO, it banked to the left and the UFO stopped moving then suddenly sped off to the right at a 45-degree angle, pinging off instantly at an incredible speed and disappearing into the night sky.

For over twenty years Neil pondered what he saw, until the so-called 'tic-tac' UFO footage captured on the cameras of a jet fighter from USS *Nimitz* during a routine flight off California in 2004 was finally officially released by the Pentagon in 2020. At last, there was what he had seen, finally captured on camera. But what the 'tic-tac' was that Neil saw (and many others who have spotted that form of UFO in our skies over the years) remains unexplained.

Mystery Lights Over Norfolk

In the early hours of Saturday 5 October 1996 unexplained lights were seen off the Norfolk coast that were recorded on radar and seen by members of the coastguard, police and public.

First reported at 3.14 a.m. as a strange and stationary red and green light south-east of Skegness, Lincolnshire, it was confirmed as a 'radar contact' just minutes later by RAF Kinloss and RAF Neatishead, and there were not meant to be any military or civil flights in the area. The North Sea tanker MV *Conocoast* confirmed to Great Yarmouth Coastguard they had 'these lights on visual, now they are flashing red, green and white' and added: 'Cannot identify it as an aircraft as it looks stationary and is approximately 1 mile high.'

Yarmouth Coastguard recorded the conversation that subsequently transpired:

> Yarmouth Coastguard: 'Did you see from which direction it appeared?'
>
> *Concoast*: It just appeared and is stationary
>
> 03.53
> Kinloss: Neatishead say it could be caused by the weather
>
> Coastguard: I don't think so we have visual contact
>
> Kinloss: Well, Neatishead and Northwood report there is no transponder on this object and therefore no means of interrogation. It is obvious that whatever it is it does not want anyone to know that it is there. Also Neatishead report its position as directly over Boston.

04.08
Conocoast: It is still stationary and flashing red, green, blue and white. It looks very high north of us, and there is no engine noise.

04.17
Coastguard: Skegness can you get video footage as the RAF are very interested and may require it later.

04.27
Kinloss: Neatishead are keeping a log of what looks like clutter on the radar.

04.45
Coastguard: *Conocoast*, can you give us an update?

Conocoast: We can see two lights flashing green and red.

05.01
Coastguard: Give us both bearings of the two lights.

Conocoast: There is one stationary light at 345 deg true and the other at 160 true. The lights are both visible with the naked eye and both exhibit the same characteristics flashing red, blue, green and white.

05.17
Boston police: We can still see the light. It is towards the south-east and seems about 40-45 degrees up in the sky ... it is just a bright light to us.

05.21
Kinloss: Neatishead are running a trace on this and cannot explain it. If they are helicopters they are fast approaching the end of their endurance and it is well over two hours since the first report let alone how long they were up there before they were actually sighted.

05.52
Conocoast: We can still see the lights and they are on their original bearings and flashing the same colours but they seem higher and dimmer.

07.08
Flt Lt McFarlane, Neatishead: We had a report from Northwood that a civil flight had also reported strange lights in the area. They fit exactly what was seen from the ground, multi-coloured flashing lights.

07.31
Flt Lt George, Northwood: This echo is still on our screens and we cannot explain this at all apart from it being a meteorological phenomena but then again we have visual sightings as well. The civilian flight that reported these lights as a flare was six miles away at the time. All very strange.

11.09
Neatishead: The object still has not moved, London radar and Waddington can also see it.

Despite later denials from RAF sources that no Air Force aircraft had been scrambled to investigate because the objects were not considered as any threat, a military jet had been spotted heading towards the lights at 9 a.m. on Saturday morning.

At 7.20 p.m., Anglia radar reported nothing was visible. It was also around this time that the cause of the mysterious lights that had been seen by multiple witnesses began to be attributed to Boston Stump.

Flt Lt Keith Sweatman told a reporter: 'As far as we were aware, there was no aircraft activity in that area – there was certainly no exercises on,' but added he believed the radar return had bounced from the 273-foot spire of St Botolph's Church in Boston, commonly known as 'Boston Stump' in Lincolnshire and created a 'permanent echo' on the screens.

The Prestwick Airport Incident

Declassified MoD files released in 2010 revealed a case recorded in February 1999 of an air traffic controller at Prestwick Airport who tracked a high-speed UFO moving across his radar screen. An extensive investigation by RAF air defence staff was instigated as a result and the radar tapes were impounded. An official report in the file concluded 'no additional evidence could be found to corroborate what the air traffic controller had spotted'.

Chapter 7

From 2000 to the Present

Lincolnshire Wind Turbine Wrecked by UFO?

On Sunday 4 January 2008 a 21.9-metre-tall (72-foot) wind turbine at Fen Farm, Conisholme, Louth, Lincolnshire, was found wrecked with one of its 20-metre (66-foot) blades torn off and another wrecked by whatever had collided with it. Metal fatigue, a pilotless stealth aircraft, lightning, falling ice from an aircraft or an adjoining turbine blade and even a meteorite were all suggested as possible causes for the crash, but there was simply no evidence to back up any of these suggestions. Several local people, however, claimed they had seen mysterious lights in the sky near the wind farm at 4 a.m. Among them was turkey farmer and county councillor Robert Palmer of Saltfleetby, who saw 'a round, white light with tentacles that seemed to be hovering in the area'.

Dale Vince, the founder of the renewable energy company Ecotricity, who own the turbines, commented on BBC Radio 4's *Today* programme that whatever had hit the blades had been 'The size and weight of a cow', but it was reported that no wreckage of whatever hit the turbine had been recovered from the scene. Fraser McLachlan, the chief executive of GCube who insure over 25,000 wind turbines worldwide, also commented: 'Such incidents occur five or six times a year.'

Police Helicopter Chases UFO

A South Wales Police Air Support Unit helicopter and its three-man crew was hovering at 500 feet awaiting clearance to land at the Ministry of Defence base at St Athan, near Cardiff, at 12.40 a.m. on 8 June 2008 when it was forced to take evasive action by banking sharply to avoid being hit by a 'flying saucer-shaped' craft that came directly towards them at high speed from below. The pilot of the police helicopter then gave chase, pursing the object that travelled at incredible speed over the Bristol Channel until they were over the North Devon coast when they lost sight of it. Running low on fuel they had no other option than to give up the pursuit and head back. Cardiff International Airport air traffic control provided a service to the police helicopter to ensure it had appropriate air space to St Athan to refuel.

The story attracted local and national media attention and initially a police spokesman went on record, stating: 'We can confirm the Air Support Unit sighted an unusual aircraft. This was reported to the relevant authorities for investigation ... They are convinced it was a UFO. It sounds far-fetched, but they know what they saw.'

Despite a number of witnesses coming forward who had watched the incident from the ground, a later statement was issued to the press by South Wales Police that denied their helicopter gave chase, claiming instead that the matter had been inaccurately reported in the media. Subsequent requests made under the Freedom of Information Act to the Civil Aviation Authority and Ministry of Defence have received responses from both organisations claiming they 'have no knowledge of the incident'.

UFO Encounters Near Church Stretton

The journey along the Burway, near Church Stretton, that leads to a plateau on the high ground among the hills of the Long Mynd in Shropshire affords some of the finest views across the surrounding countryside by day and lovely dark skies with no light pollution that are perfect for viewing the stars at night. The winding roadway around the hillsides is also steep and narrow with room for only one car in places, with buttock-clenching sheer drops on one side. It is the sort of road you really hope you will not meet any vehicle coming in the opposite direction. But when crossing this lonely road at night some people have encountered unexplained objects from above.

There have been sightings of UFOs in this area since the 1960s, either bright, moving and hovering lights or bright, illuminated craft in the air. When the author of this book investigated UFO activity in the area he found more people from Stretton and the surrounding towns and villages had seen the lights and craft than had gone on record to report them, fearing ridicule if they did so.

In Phil Hoyle's UFO casebook on the Shropshire Live website, he recounts the story of local mechanic Tony Foster who was crossing the Burway at between 12.30 and 1 a.m. one dark night in 1990. As he crossed the plateau he became aware of a light descending from the sky when suddenly it was above his car, sending down a dazzling beam of light. The moment the light engulfed the car his engine stopped dead and would not restart. He got out of his car, probably wondering if it was a helicopter above him, but as he did so he felt the outside of the car seemed to be surrounded by a very high electrical static charge.

As Tony looked up, he realised the source of the light was only about 150 feet above him. As he looked at the light 'he could just make out other coloured lights that reminded him of rainbows emanating from the middle of the object'. Transfixed by the light hovering above him for about thirty seconds, it soon sank in that this really was no normal aircraft and he fled back inside his car and attempted to start the engine again, without success. He cast his eyes up towards the craft and at that moment the light went out and the UFO flew off at a phenomenal speed. His car started as if nothing had happened a few seconds later and he drove home.

Almost exactly the same thing happened to a gentleman who was driving home alone across the Burway from Church Stretton in his Volvo estate in the early hours one morning during the autumn of 2010. He is a down to earth professional man who is keen to point out he is not a massive sci-fi fan, nor does he read lots of books about UFOs. He seeks neither publicity nor financial gain. He shares this story out of public interest and in the hope that it may generate some answers as to what he experienced, on the strict understanding he remains anonymous.

As he was driving past the area of the plateau known as Devil's Mouth, now a noted Dark Skies Discovery Site, our witness became aware of an illuminated object a couple of hundred feet above him that would soon be heading over his car, or at least he was expecting to see it pass to the other side. Instead, a dazzling bright white light suddenly engulfed his car, the road and ground for several feet around it. It also stopped the car dead in its tracks. It is strange to pray for a sudden stop, but our witness did not really experience a jolt, as you might expect when suddenly applying the brakes in a car. He tried and failed to start the car, but then took a moment to gather his thoughts. As he did so, the inside of the car seemed to fill with static electricity and his ears were filled with the sound of an intense, high-pitched whine that hurt his ear drums. He then felt the car slowly and gently lifting off the road. He reached for the car door handle to get out and pulled it. It appeared to function normally, but he tried it several times with increasing desperation and the door would not open.

Then, the dazzling beam shut off as suddenly as it had flicked on, and the glowing object sped off over the hills in the direction of Stretton at an incredible speed. As the light extinguished, the car, which the driver estimated was about a foot off the ground, was dropped back on the roadway, offside wheels landing first. Everything was suddenly dark, still and eerily quiet. The intense high-pitched whine was gone, he could no longer feel any static and his car started again, first time. Although badly shaken by his experience, our witness was determined to drive home. He had only gone a short distance along the road when he encountered what appeared to be an unmarked military Land Rover travelling at speed. It slowed quickly. It did not appear to have to brake hard and bumped up the verge to let our witness pass. As he did so, a soldier in camouflage fatigues but not wearing any headwear stuck his head out of the driver's side window. He appeared stressed and asked, 'Are you ok?'

Our witness, still in some shock after what he had experienced, had already wound down his window in anticipation of some exchange. He simply replied 'Yes' and drove on, desperate to get home, as the Land Rover sped off in the direction of Stretton. To his lasting regret, our witness did not ask if the soldiers in the Land Rover had seen what had happened to him or if they had any idea what was going on. Reflecting on the incident, our witness states what he experienced 'felt absolutely surreal but was only too real'.

The Dudley Dorito

Triangular UFOs made dramatic appearances over the Black Country and Birmingham, with sightings reported at Dudley, Tipton, Wolverhampton, Hagley and Quarry Bank during the latter half of the first decade of the twenty-first century. Sightings were frequent and witnessed by numerous people in the area. The distinctive triangular shape of the UFO was equated to one of the popular snacks of the day and was soon dubbed 'The Dudley Dorito' by local people and in the press. Some of the best-reported sightings occurred during November 2010. A triangular object estimated to have been 'four or five times the size of a commercial airliner' was spotted by Dave Allen of Bendall Road, Boldmere, Sutton Coldfield near Birmingham, on 4 November 2010.

Later that same month, at around 10.15 p.m. on Sunday 14 November 2010, quality inspector Munesh Mistry (twenty-one) and his friend Neil Martin (twenty-one) spotted the triangular UFO in the skies above Mr Mistry's home on Andrew Road in Tipton, near Dudley. He described it as 'an amazing fast moving and silent craft in the shape of a triangle made up of what appeared to be three lights'. The 'Dorito' has even been captured on mobile phone camera footage when David Banner (thirty-eight) was walking home from a bus stop in the Ettingshill Park area of Wolverhampton at about 7.00 p.m. on Sunday 17 December 2010 when he spotted something 'flickering and darting' above him and he managed to grab a few seconds footage of it before it disappeared. Mr Banner went public with the footage in December 2023. Whether the UFO really is alien in origin or glimpses, as some suggest, of a terrestrial but top-secret military aircraft remains to be proved either way.

The Pentyrch Incident

In the early hours of 26 February 2016, a huge pyramid-shaped vessel, its outline ringed with bright lights, appeared over the village of Pentyrch, near Cardiff, South Wales. Witnesses had first noticed a red light in the western sky that was soon followed by more lights, which formed the outline of huge upright triangle or pyramid with a curved lower edge. As it moved through the sky the UFO appeared to be under intelligent control. No witnesses had noticed the object arrive, it just seemed to materialise (some ufologists have suggested this evinces an inter-dimensional journey).

Local resident Caz Clarke was one of those who witnessed the events first-hand. She describes how a small, bright, green-glowing object like a star probably the size of a small car appeared to be launched from the top of the pyramid. Its exact shape could not be discerned because it was so bright. It flew across the sky until it rested and rocked gently just above the tree line. Military aircraft were soon on the scene; Caz identified the first to arrive as an E3 Sentry early warning and control aircraft, or AWAC. Other military aircraft including two Hercules arrived soon afterwards from the direction of MoD St Athan and Cardiff. The green object emitted three bright flashes or strobes bobbing in the air then sped off north-west in the direction of Llantrisant followed by the four military aircraft.

Meanwhile, the pyramid has listed, turned slowly anti-clockwise and seemed to get closer and closer to the land beneath it, almost as if it was going to land. Caz became transfixed by the rays 'like thick lightning' that emitted from the UFO towards the ground; her friend Dave who was with her spotted objects that glowed a bright 'tail light red' leaving the pyramid. These soon appeared over the trees closer to the pair and could then be seen to be barrel-shaped objects which hovered silently above the fields. One of them was directly above Caz which she claims she felt 'scan' her. These objects then flew off. Very soon afterward three Apache helicopters arrived, apparently on an interception course for the green-glowing object spotted earlier. About ten minutes later there was a loud explosion from the direction of Llantrisant whereupon people were shaken awake in their beds and car alarms were set off. Data from British Geological Survey at Monmouth also recorded a seismological anomaly had occurred that night.

More aircraft, identified as C-17 gunships, Chinooks and attack helicopters, followed soon afterwards. Llantrisant residents were used to military aircraft from the RAF St Athan base, but the activity in the air above them was like nothing they had seen or heard before. Concerns were also raised by the low-flying military aircraft and the number of military vehicles that suddenly concentrated on the area, and nearby several residents called the police. People attempting to travel the main roads and major highways of the area found they were closed off and police manning the roadblocks blamed an overturned lorry for the closure. This really does beg the question: could a single overturned lorry really cause so many roads to be closed off? Residents also spoke of hearing two loud explosions: one in the air and one on the ground in the area of Llantrisant Forest, known to locals as Smilog Woods, about 4 miles west of Pentyrch.

When daylight came, several local people went to investigate what had happened in the woodland where they thought they had seen the UFO brought down. They were shocked to discover freshly broken and smashed 40-foot conifers that had been severed mid-trunk, which appeared to indicate the passage of some large aircraft smashing through them, but no wreckage was discovered. In the aftermath of the incident official sources soon attempted to quash the concerns of there being any UFO activity over South Wales by claiming what people had witnessed was a military exercise.

Soon afterwards rows of tents appeared on a field on a farm near the crash site and a team of as yet unidentified personnel in civilian clothes and tents appeared to undertake a fingertip search and surveyed the area. They remained there for several weeks into March 2016. A search of Llantrisant Common for metal fragments also appears to have been carried out. The damaged woods and the field where Caz and her friend witnessed the rays of 'thick lighting' emitted by the UFO had areas that appeared to have suffered heat damage and remained 'bald' or suffered stunted growth since the incident. Radiation readings taken from these areas have also shown to be higher than should be expected.

In response to the Freedom of Information request in 2019 specifically asking about the pyramid craft and other objects spotted in the sky that night, the MoD admitted they hold information related to the request but claimed a qualified exception under Section 26 (Defence) of the Freedom of Information Act, citing 'operational sensitivity' and stating 'the public interest in maintaining the exception outweighs the public interest in disclosure'.

So, the question remains: what was witnessed in the sky above Pentyrch? The Ministry of Defence have always maintained it was simply a training exercise between the RAF and British Army, known as Exercise Chameleon. Alternatively, did the RAF intercept a UFO and shoot it down into Smilog Woods? And could this then have been recovered by the military during the early hours of 26 February 2016 and, by denial and refusal to disclose what really happened to the public, created the greatest UFO cover-up of the twenty-first century?

Select Bibliography and Suggested Further Reading

Books

Blundell, Nigel and Boar, Roger, *The World's Greatest UFO Mysteries* (Octopus Books, 1983)

Butler, Brenda, Street, Dot and Randles, Jenny, *Sky Crash: A Cosmic Conspiracy* (Neville Spearman, 1984)

Chapman, Robert, *UFO: Flying Saucers Over Britain?* (Granada, 1968)

Clark, Caz and Jones, Gari, *The Pentyrch Incident: The Greatest UFO Cover-up of Modern Times* (Independently Published, 2021)

Gibbons, Gavin, *The Coming of the Space Ships* (Neville Spearman, 1956)

Gleaves, Jason, *UFO Encounters* (Flying Disk Press, 2022)

Ingleby, Holcombe, *The Zeppelin Raid in West Norfolk* (Arnold, 1915)

Jones, R. V., *Most Secret War* (Hamish Hamilton, 1978)

Jones Pugh, Randall and Holiday F. W., *The Dyfed Enigma* (Faber & Faber, 1979)

Mantle, Philip, *UFO Landings UK* (Flying Disk Press, 2022)

Nagaitis, Carl and Mantle, Philip, *Without Consent: A Comprehensive Survey of Missing Time and Abduction Phenomena in the UK* (Ringpull Press, 1994)

Paget, Peter, *UFO-UK* (New English Library, 1980)

Price, Robert, *UFOs over Hampshire and the Isle of Wight* (Ensign Publications, 1999)

Redfern, Nick, *Cosmic Crashes* (Simon & Schuster, 1999)

Regan, Pat, *UFO The Search for Truth* (Can Write, 2010)

Shuttlewood, Arthur, *The Flying Saucerers* (Sphere, 1976)

Shuttlewood, Arthur, *The Warminster Mystery* (1967)

Shuttlewood, Arthur, *UFO Magic in Motion* (Sphere, 1979)

Shuttlewood, Arthur, *More UFOs over Warminster* (Arthur Barker, 1979)

Stanway, Roger and Pace, Anthony R., *Flying Saucer Report* (Newchapel Observatory, 1968)

Trench, Brinsley Le Poer, *The Flying Saucer Story* (Neville Spearman, 1966)

Watson, Brian, *Some Kind of Club A History of No 6 Group ROC Norwich* (DJ Asociates, 1984)

Whittington Egan, Richard, *'Weekend' Book of Ghosts and Horror No. 2* (Harmsworth 1982)

Wilkins, Harold T., *Flying Saucers on the Moon* (Peter Owen, 1954)

Newspapers

Daily Express
Daily Herald
Daily Mail
Daily News
Eastern Daily Press
Eastern Evening News
Illustrated Chronicle
Illustrated London News
Kentish Express
Newcastle Evening Chronicle
Newcastle Journal
News Chronicle
Northern Echo
Peterborough Citizen and Advertiser
Runcorn Weekly News
Sheffield Star
Shropshire Star
Stanley News
Sunday Despatch
Sunday Sun
Sunderland Echo
The Times
Wandsworth Borough News
Warminster Journal
Woking News

Wolverhampton Express and Star
Worcester Evening News
Yorkshire Post

Magazines

BUFORA Journal
COS-MOS
Flying Saucer News
Flying Saucer Review
Fortean Times
LUFORO Bulletin
Northern UFO News
Omni
Orbit
Skysearch
The Unexplained
UFO Bulletin
UFO Info
UFOLOG Information Sheet
UFO Magazine
Uranus
X-Factor

Websites

BBC News Online, bbc.co.uk/news
britishnewspaperarchive.co.uk
David Toms TV, youtube.com/watch?v=tkLv_DYxiyQ
'Pentyrch: The greatest UFO cover up of the 21st century?', herald.wales (2 October 2023)
'Phil Hoyle Shropshire UFO Casebook Part 7 The Long Mynd UFO', shropshirelive.com (12 October 2023)
The Paranormal Scholar, youtube.com/watch?v=VJTGpxOqzjA

Acknowledgements

The author would like to express his personal thanks to the following archives, libraries and individuals for their help and encouragement of this book: The National Archives, Newcastle Local Studies Library, Tyneside UFO Society Archive, Bentwaters Cold War Museum, RAF Air Defence Radar Museum, Neatishead, Norfolk Heritage Centre, Norfolk and Norwich Millennium Library, Norfolk Record Office, Chloe Baker-Cooper, Brenda Butler, Dave Schrader, Jason Gleaves, Colonel Charles I. Halt USAF (retired), Philip and Ronald Kinsella, David Hepworth, Sarah Mulligan, Derek Tree, Debbie Moore, Abbie Moore, Michelle Bullivant, Stewart. P. Evans, Kerry Freeman, Nick Grant and all the team at Amberley Publishing. Last but by no means least, I thank my family for their enduring love and support.

The author would also like to extend his heartfelt thanks to everyone who has shared snippets, stories and scrapbooks of UFO material with him over the years.